FILM POSTERS
SCIENCE FICTION

FILM POSTERS
SCIENCE FICTION

edited by tony nourmand and graham marsh
foreword by professor sir christopher frayling

EVERGREEN

It! The Terror From Beyond Space (1958)
US 41 x 27 in. (104 x 69 cm)

Plan 9 From Outer Space (1959)
US 41 x 27 in. (104 x 69 cm)

EVERGREEN is an imprint of
TASCHEN GmbH

© 2006 TASCHEN GmbH
Hohenzollernring 53, D-50672 Köln
www.taschen.com

ISBN 978-3-8228-5627-7

Printed in Singapore

Text by Tony Nourmand and Alison Aitchison
Art direction and design by Graham Marsh
Research and Co-ordination by Alison Aitchison
Page layout by Trevor Gray
Proof-reading by Roxanna Hajiani
Principal photography by A.J. Photographics

Unless otherwise stated, all images used in this book are from
The Reel Poster Archive.

ACKNOWLEDGEMENTS

Tarek AbuZayyad, Richard & Barbara Allen, Farhad Amirahmadi,
Austrian National Library, Department of Broadsheets, Poster and Ex Libris,
Tim Bradshaw, Martin Bridgewater, Joe Burtis, Glyn Callingham,
Jean-Louis Capitaine, José Ma. Carpio, Philip Castle, Ciné-Images,
Anne Coco, Andrew Cohen, Mark Faulkner, Greg Ferland, Film Museum, Berlin,
Leslie Gardner, Armando Giuffrida, John Goddard, Helmut Hamm, Kirk Hammett,
Yoshikazu Inoue, Eric & Prim Jean-Baptiste, Laurence Johns, Andy Johnson,
Mike Kaplan, John & Billie Kisch, Peter & Betty Langs, James Lavelle, Sean Lee,
Andrew MacDonald, Krzysztof Marcinkiewicz, June Marsh, Philip Masheter,
James Moores, Ian A. Nabeshima, Tomoaki 'Nigo' Nagao, Andrew Nicholau-
Creative Partnership, Gaspar Noe, The Nouvelle Vague Collection, Susan Pack,
Rancho Santa Fe, CA, author of Film Posters of the Russian Avant-Garde,
Sergio Pignatone, Martin Pope, Robert Jess Roth, Separate Cinema,
Steve Smith, Dan Strebin, The Crew from the Island, Andreas Timmer,
Steve & Kanella Wilson and Kim Goddard.

Special thanks to Bruce Marchant, without whose help these books would
not be possible.

Conquest Of Space (1955)
US 41 × 27 in. (104 × 69 cm)

CONTENTS

FOREWORD

The gala première of Fritz Lang's *Frau Im Mond/Woman In The Moon* in October 1929 must have been quite something. The frontage of the UFA Palace cinema in Berlin was covered with a gigantic animated panel, showing the earth and the moon against a starry sky and a rocket making round trips between them. That same day, newspapers speculated about the possible launch of a rocket into the stratosphere by Professor Hermann Oberth of Nürnberg, technical adviser to Lang's film. And the poster, showing a snub-nosed rocket powered by mixing and burning alcohol (as a liquid fuel) and liquid oxygen (as an oxidizer), hurtling diagonally through the heavens shortly after countdown, was all over the west end of Berlin. It was a publicist's dream. The rumour about Oberth's rocket turned out to be part of the advertising package.

This was the first time anywhere the general public had seen a visual representation of a liquid-fuel rocket (up to then, diagrams had been confined to specialist books such as Oberth's *Rocket Into Interplanetary Space*) and in the movie itself the first time anyone, even the specialists, had seen a countdown. Up until then, cinematic moon-shots had tended to belong to the Jules Verne/Georges Méliès school of 'space guns': more a question of ballistics than of rocket science. Or else they took the form of giant black-powder rockets. Before *Frau Im Mond*, the countdown was a less dramatic count up.

Buck Rogers first appeared, in comic-strip form, that same year. The first serious space odyssey film coincided with the first major American science-fiction comic series. A few years later, in the movies, Buck would travel in a flat, triangular metal spaceship with fire coming out of exhausts in its tail. Flash Gordon (from a rival comic strip) preferred a more bulbous silver machine puffing fire and smoke. In *Rocket Ship* (1938), Buster Crabbe's spacecraft had wings and little exhaust pipes. All these concepts were partly inspired by the covers of popular interwar pulp magazines such as *Amazing Stories, Astounding Science Fiction* and *Fantastic Adventures*. And of course by *Frau Im Mond*, except that they took off and landed from a horizontal position. While Buck Rogers tried to save Saturn for democracy in the 25th century by thwarting the evil Killer Kane, and Flash Gordon stopped Ming the Merciless from doing dreadful things to Dale Arden on the planet Mongo, H. G. Wells was busy preparing his weighty 'reply' to Fritz Lang's *Metropolis* and *Woman In The Moon: Things To Come*.

Already, science fiction was going in two separate directions: westerns set in the zero gravity of space, where the cowboys (usually played by Buster Crabbe) wore tight-fitting dude-ranch shirts and studded belts and the Indians had eight eyes and enlarged craniums; and serious – in the case of *Things To Come*, painfully serious – films which, like the best of predictive literature, thought hard about the philosophy and politics of science as well as the hardware, the social structures of the future as well as the action. Wells's reply to Fritz Lang involved, at the climax of *Things To Come*, a huge Space Gun – mirroring the anti-aircraft gun used in the opening air-raid sequence – which propels the young couple into outer space: this optimistic

ending would, apparently, 'balance the first war crescendo'; guns could be used for war, and they could also be used for peace. Which shall it be? The Space Gun was, even at the time, treated with the same kind of derision as greeted the character in *Destination Moon* (1950, technical adviser Hermann Oberth again) who said, 'It'll never get off the ground – no propellers.' The publicity people on *Things To Come*, quick to spot something the audience might laugh at, redrew the posters to show a sleek rocket ship with speed trails coming out of its tail – visually separated from the big gun, which now looked like a long-range cannon. On this rare and possibly unique occasion, the poster was more scientifically accurate than the film it was promoting.

By the time of *Destination Moon* – the one where a retired American General raises sponsorship for the development of a nuclear-powered rocket by predicting that 'the first country that can use the moon for the launching of missiles will control the earth' – the visual conventions for depicting rockets (souped-up versions of the pencil-shaped wartime V2) and the lunar landscape had settled down. The astronauts even wore insulated space-suits. Chesley Bonestell, who had recently provided the visuals for Willy Ley's book *Conquest Of Space* (1949) and who was about to produce a classic series of illustrations of space travel for *Collier's* magazine, provided credible artwork for *Destination Moon*: he chose as the actual destination a crater on the northern latitudes of the moon, from which the earth could be seen near the horizon. Georges Méliès had first shown this effect at the turn of the century, in his vaudeville parody of Jules Verne; Bonestell made it look hyper-real.

The popular success of *Destination Moon* – and of the following year's *The Day The Earth Stood Still*, with its message about the responsible use of the atomic bomb and its imagery of the all-powerful robot policeman Gort with his opening visor and devastating single eye-beam – led to more movies in a similar vein. Documentary look, interesting design, ethical dilemma.

Bonestell worked again with producer George Pal on *When Worlds Collide, War Of The Worlds* (the spindly walking tripods of the original novel becoming flying saucers with protruding stalks) and *The Conquest Of Space* (the Mars landscape as red and chunky – 'two years in the making'). *Conquest* was based on a book by Wernher von Braun – the man who during the Second World War had been technical director of the Nazi V2 project at Peenemünde on the Baltic coast, resulting in the world's first ballistic missile, before surrendering to American troops in Bavaria two days after Hitler's suicide – and the manned space station which orbits the earth in the film, plus the outsized spaceship, were built like massive battle cruisers, precursors of the spacecraft which have filled the screen since *Star Wars* and which constantly remind us that the force is with us rather than the guys in the coalscuttle helmets thanks to superior technical know-how. But *Conquest* was a box-office disaster. Together with the big overspends on the special effects of *Forbidden Planet*, and the high cost of creating the planetscape of Altair IV, it put

Frau Im Mond (Woman In The Moon) (1929)
German 86 × 40 in. (210 × 97 cm)
Art by Alfred Herrman
Courtesy of the Film Museum, Berlin

Hollywood off serious and remotely realistic science fiction until *2001: A Space Odyssey* in 1968.

Conquest Of Space included the celebrated line 'There are some things that man is not meant to do', spoken in all seriousness. In the golden treasury of science-fiction one-liners, this is up there with 'It's a crazy idea but it just might work', 'He's fleeing from what we call civilization', 'Is it a bird, is it a plane, or is it ...?' and of course 'Klaatu barado nikto'; it has long since entered the dictionaries of movie phrases as one of the defining quotations of the genre. In fact, it would have been more in place in one of the many ensuing low-to-very-low-budget films about secret atomic science leading to unintended side-effects – which required the military (a new element in such movies) to destroy the resulting giant ants or spiders or flies or scorpions or mantises or reptiles or moles or crabs or cats which threatened Eisenhower's middle America. Sometimes the threat came from the desert or the greenhouse or from the bottom of the lagoon. Or from the skies, which just went to show that you had to keep watching them. Sometimes the threat took human form, which was particularly sneaky – like in *Invasion Of The Body Snatchers* (1956). Often, the threat was called 'It' – not 'He' or 'She' but 'It'. *It Came From Outer Space* (in 3D), *It Conquered The World*, *It Stalked The Ocean Floor* and *It Came From Beneath The Sea* – a film about a giant octopus, contaminated by radiation, which terrorizes San Francisco, only it is in fact a sextopus since the budget could only manage six tentacles. *It! The Terror From Beyond Space* (1958) – a stowaway alien on a spaceship returning from Mars which 'feeds on blood and bone' – was the origin of the storyline for *Alien*: in the Ridley Scott/Hans Rudi Giger version the gill-man in a rubber suit was to become a giant bio-mechanical prawn-being which spits battery fluid at all comers and reminds the crew of the Nostromo that 'in space no-one can hear you scream'.

Disappointingly, a proposed sequel to *Them!* – to be called *It, Son Of Them!*, which would have been one of the all-time great titles – was never made.

But *Them!* (1954), a huge box-office success for Warners, was the film which started the trend: the combination of a quasi-documentary cinematic style with a story about atomic tests in the desert leading to the creation of giant mutant ants as a by-product was evidently a winning one. The film even included a suitably apocalyptic Biblical epigram: 'And there shall be destruction and darkness over creation. And the beasts shall rule over the earth.' The poster showed the beasts, full-face – red-eyed ants with serrated antennae, pushing into diagonal letters blaring the word T-H-E-M, complete with a message in a cartoon bubble, 'Kill one and two take its place!', flames and a tank. Thanks to the success of the formula, the beasts were to rule over the earth for the rest of the decade and beyond – combining post A-bomb and H-bomb fears about lingering radiation, the red menace, and a new paranoia about hygiene in the home. In the age of the all-electric kitchen, the bulging refrigerator and the post-war consumer boom, some of the audience's deepest fears seem to have been about

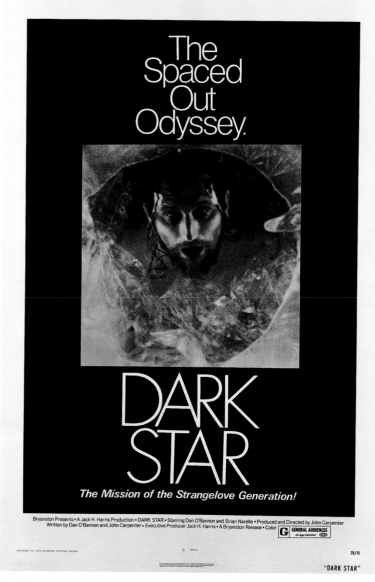

Dark Star (1974)
US 41 × 27 in. (104 × 69 cm)
Courtesy of the Martin Bridgewater Collection

he revenge of the creepy-crawlies. *The Incredible Shrinking Man* (1957) pits the ever-decreasing hero against a large household cat and a spider, using only a needle and thread, a pair of scissors and a matchbox as weapons. When all else failed, the new gadgets turned out to be no use at all.

The posters and graphics for these 'mobilization against the mutants' films have become, like the covers of some interwar pulps, among the most celebrated visuals in the genre: big letters, with exclamation marks, against a dark or fiery background; the colour yellow connoting fear or anxiety; a mutant/alien carrying a scantily clad heroine in its arms or jaws (they may have been called 'It' but they usually behaved like 'He'); a terrified crowd running towards the viewer in the foreground; some grandiose high-impact claims about the thrills in store such as 'He walks through walls' or 'You'll see it tear a city apart' or 'The biggest thing since creation' or 'The science monster who would destroy the world' or 'Out of primordial depths to destroy the world' or a 'Co-ed beauty captive of man monster' or 'A beautiful woman by day – a lusting queen wasp by night'.

It took *2001* to bring the seriousness back, in the year before the first real-life astronaut took a giant step on to the moon. Based on an

Arthur C. Clarke novella – just as *Destination Moon* had been based on a Robert Heinlein story for children – it also brought a new surface realism. Stanley Kubrick was at pains to put over the 'everyday nature of space travel' thirty-three years on, and he employed Harry Lange – who had worked on the future concepts scheme at NASA in the 1950s – to help him achieve it. Lange and his team were responsible for creating spacecraft which satisfied Kubrick's incessant search for justification and verisimilitude. The pencil-shaped rockets of the early 1950s made way for a vast rotating space station and – perhaps the most influential shot in the film – the spacecraft *Discovery* slowly gliding against a background of infinity across the width of the Cinerama screen. Lange was to recall that Kubrick originally said to him, 'I can get better illustrators a dime a dozen, but they don't have your background.' The cool, NASA-inspired design of everything from costumes and interiors to vehicles, was reflected in the poster with its clear 1960s typography and photo-realist artwork. This publicity did not shout at the audience, and it did not need exclamation marks.

I can remember seeing the Cinerama version of *2001* at the London Pavilion. I was sitting in the front row, and someone just behind me was smoking a joint. The 'Beyond Infinity' section with its faster-than-light drive through space induced a kind of delirious visual overload. This did not make the ending any more comprehensible – why was Keir Dulka reborn as a star child, and why as an old man was he walking around what looked like an eighteenth-century hotel room? – but it made for a memorably cinematic experience. Perhaps this was why, when *2001* was reissued, it was re-branded as 'the Ultimate Trip' – a tagline which was to be parodied by *Dark Star* (1974) as 'bombed out in space' and 'The Spaced Out Odyssey'. The squeaky clean interiors of *2001* became the messy and student-y cockpit of *Dark Star*, which in turn became the tramp steamer travelling home through space in *Alien*.

There are many other treasures in this book. Jane Fonda in tights, kinky boots, big hair and a protruding breastplate on the US poster for *Barbarella* (1968) – the less cool, more funky side of 'the swinging 1960s'. The extraordinary Polish poster by Eryk Lipinski for *Planet Of The Apes* (also 1968), which gives away the movie's punch line but produces a classic piece of graphic design in the process. The fascinatingly different German and American campaigns for *Metropolis* (1926): the former is taken from the film, complete with the robot Maria and deco lettering; the latter introduces a proto-skyscraper in distended gothic cathedral style, captured by searchlights, which are not in the film. The poster for Jean-Luc Godard's *Alphaville* (1965), with Eddie Constantine in a trench-coat as Peter Cheyney's detective Lemmy Caution – for some obscure reason, there was a cult of Cheyney among French crime-novel buffs – and with an alienating new-build Paris suburb in the background, doubling as a rainy city of the future.

Science Fiction Poster Art has been compiled by Tony Nourmand and Graham Marsh with their usual thoroughness, care and expertise.

Creatures created in a poster gallery! Can nothing stop it? See the attack of the graphic designers! Amazing!

In other words *It, Son Of Them* has at last arrived.

Christopher Frayling
April 2003

Planet Of The Apes (Planeta Malp) (1968)
Polish 33 × 23 in. (84 × 58 cm)
Art by Eryk Lipinski
Courtesy of The Reel Poster Gallery

THE SHAPE OF THINGS THAT CAME …

Becoming involved in the science-fiction project was a real eye-opener for us. The material turned out to be very different to our initial expectations – and certainly exceeded them dramatically. It may be that the very nature of science fiction itself – the imaginative exuberance that is its lifeblood – offers artists greater inspiration and more creative opportunities than other genres.

One thing that soon became apparent is that most writers of science fiction stick to their lasts, you do not find Jules Verne or Philip K. Dick straying into romance, comedy or drama. Perhaps this is because science fiction offers the writer the scope to incorporate elements of all these. In contrast, the directors, illustrators and artists whose work is discussed and illustrated in this book come from surprisingly diverse backgrounds. In fact, many of the more interesting science-fiction films were made by directors with no previous experience in the genre. The most notable example is Stanley Kubrick's (1928–1999) *2001: A Space Odyssey* (1968), which remains a seminal and landmark science-fiction masterpiece.

There are no hard and fast rules when it comes to the artists behind science-fiction film posters. Robert T. McCall, responsible for the Cinerama poster campaign for *2001*, is famous for his paintings of space that document NASA's history. But *2001* is his only film poster. In contrast, the legendary designer Saul Bass has been responsible for a host of film posters, yet *Seconds* (1966) is his only venture into science fiction. Likewise, the unusual, Style B, American 81 × 81 inch poster for *World Without End* (1956) is the only science-fiction poster by Alberto Vargas, famous for his pin-up illustrations of the all-American girl.

The variety of styles and designs from around the world is considerable – as illustrated by the three very different posters for *The Time Machine* (1960) featured in the book. Nonetheless, similarities in technique and approach can be identified in the work of artists from the same country. American and British artists favour a more traditional approach, as seen in Reynold Brown's design. Likewise, the French and the Italians tend to share a fairly classic, painterly style, exemplified by Silvano Campeggi's poster. (They do, however, occasionally deviate from the norm to create something out of the ordinary, as with Renato Fratini's futuristic artwork for *Invaders From Mars* (1953).) Marian Stachurski's design shows the more abstract and conceptual treatment favoured by Eastern European poster artists; the Romanian poster for *Planet Of The Apes* and Witold Dybowski's Polish poster for *Return Of The Jedi* (1983) are other examples of this style.

Science Fiction Poster Art is the first in a series of genre-based books. Although by no means intended as a definitive catalogue of science-fiction film posters, we hope this small selection provides a rich and varied flavour of what is out there.

Tony Nourmand and **Graham Marsh**

June 2003

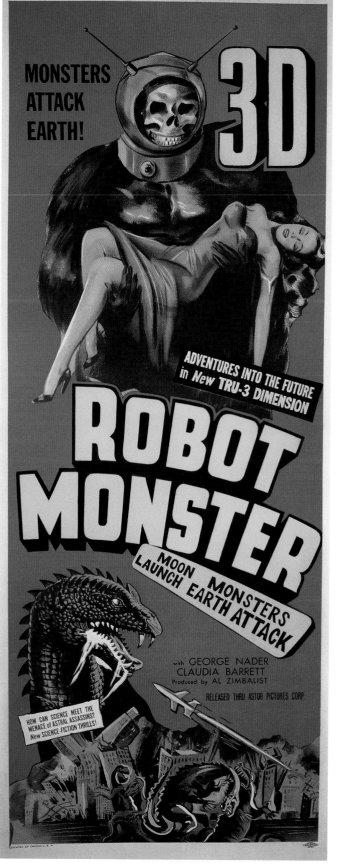

Robot Monster (1953)
US 36 × 14 in. (91 × 36 cm)

Robinson Crusoe On Mars (S.O.S. Naufragio Nello Spazio) (1964)
Italian 55 × 39 in. (140 × 99 cm)
Art by Marcello Colizzi
Courtesy of The Reel Poster Gallery

L' Avventure Straordinarissime Di Saturnino Farandola (1914)
Italian 79 × 55 in. (201 × 140 cm)
Art by Albert Robida
Courtesy of The Reel Poster Gallery

Jules Verne (1828–1905) is the father of science fiction and one of the most widely read novelists in the world. His ideas were always grandiose: he eagerly looked forward to the day when men would explore the moon, fly round the world and journey to the centre of the earth. But although his plots seemed extravagantly futuristic at the time, they were usually firmly grounded in current scientific trends. Among the many developments that he correctly predicted were helicopters, airships, rockets, submarines, cinema with sound, television … the list is long. His novels adapted perfectly for the big screen and from Georges Méliès to the present day, his books have remained a lasting, popular source of cinematic inspiration.

- **1783**. Montgolfier brothers demonstrate feasibility of hot-air balloons.
- **1903**. Wright brothers achieve first powered flight.
- **1909**. Robert Peary and Matthew Henson are the first men to reach the North Pole over land.

Frenchman **Albert Robida** (1848–1926) was a draughtsman, caricaturist and novelist. He illustrated for a number of magazines and books before establishing his own publication, *La Caricature*, with Georges Decaux. A contemporary of Jules Verne, his prophetic visions of the future are equally inspiring and he predicted many twentieth-century advances with amazing accuracy. An 1883 illustration depicts a television reporter in 1963 covering a guerrilla war in North Africa, which is watched simultaneously by a family thousands of miles away looking at a full-colour, wall-mounted display in their living room. His artwork for *L'Avventure Straordinarissime Di Saturnino Farandola* imagines chemical and underwater warfare, ideas that would again be realized in the ensuing years (minus the sea creatures). Although these are serious topics, Robida manages to capture elements of humour in the battle and the poster is characteristic of a wicked wit that pervades his work.

À La Conquête Du Pôle Nord (1907)
French 50 × 32 in. (117 × 76 cm)
Courtesy of Ciné-Images

Les Mystères Du Ciel (1912)
French 63 × 47 in. (160 × 119 cm)
Art by Caplen

Georges Méliès (1861–1938) was a pioneer of early cinema. A contemporary of the Lumière brothers, his training as an illusionist and his ownership of a theatre left him in a perfect position to take advantage of the new developments in cinematography. Méliès pioneered the use of double exposure, the split screen shot and the dissolve. His work paved the way for much that followed and the basic techniques he developed were still being used in films such as *Star Wars* (1977).

In the early 1900s, in contrast to his contemporaries who were confining their efforts to factual films, Méliès used his imagination and experience as a conjuror to produce *Voyage Dans La Lune* (1902). This fourteen-minute masterpiece was inspired by Jules Verne's *From The Earth To The Moon* (1865) and H. G. Wells' *First Men In The Moon* (1901) and includes one of cinema's most famous images of the moon grimacing after the rocket lands in its eye. Méliès also directed *À La Conquête Du Pôle* (also known as *À La Conquête Du Pôle Nord*) in 1912. This was again based on a Jules Verne novel, *Voyages Et Aventures Du Capitaine Hatteras* (1866). The colourful French poster for the film reflects Verne's and Méliès' wonderful visions: the flying machine is an amazing hybrid of dragon, stagecoach and automobile.

À La Conquête Du Pôle (1912)
French 63 × 47 in. (160 × 119 cm)
Courtesy of Ciné-Images

L'ALLIANCE CINÉMATOGRAPHIQUE EUROPÉENNE
PRÉSENTE UNE PRODUCTION UFA
RÉALISÉ PAR
FRITZ LANG
D'APRÈS LE SCÉNARIO DE
THEA VON HARBOU:

Metropolis (1962)
French 92 x 122 in. (224 x 304 cm)
Art by Boris Bilinsky
Courtesy of the Film Museum, Berlin

Boris Bilinsky

Metropolis (1926)
US 36 × 14 in. (91 × 36 cm)

With a budget of between five and eight million Deutsch Marks and 310 days of filming spread over seventeen month, Fritz Lang's *Metropolis* is the first full-length science fiction film. Under the Weimar Republic, the arts, including cinema, flourished in Germany; indeed, in the decade following the First World War, the country was the biggest centre for commercial film-making in the world, with UFA leading the way. Building on the success of *Das Kabinett Des Dr. Caligari* (1919), *Metropolis* was a gargantuan venture even for UFA.

With its colossal production costs, the film very nearly bankrupted the firm and received bad reviews when it was released. Over time, however, the significance of *Metropolis*, both as a film, and as a work of science fiction, has come to be widely appreciated and it is now recognized as a seminal work.

The film is set in 2000, when society is made up of a gigantic slave force governed by a small, capitalist elite. The contrast between the two ways of life is highlighted by a number of means; above ground, the capitalists cavort in wide, open spaces, enjoying freedom in the fresh air; meanwhile, below the surface, the strictly regimented labour force shuffles shoulder to shoulder in suffocating regimentation. The contrast between light and dark is used to great effect and much of the camerawork is innovatory, expressing sentiments in a new way by, for example, moving slowly towards the characters to express tenderness. Lang even used the inter-titles to enhance the mood – they fall down the screen as the workers go below ground or rise as the scene switches to the elite on the surface. Music is also important in the film, for example the funeral march is used as the workers' theme.

Metropolis is perhaps most famous for its cityscape. The city of the future was dominated by monumental skyscrapers and gigantic steel structures, and was based on the construction of Manhattan that was taking shape in the 1920s; a critic observed at the time that Lang's film 'serves the boldest dreams of architecture'. This vision of the towering metropolis of the future is reflected in the poster designs from around the world and has also had a direct influence on a number of films, most notably *Blade Runner* (1982) and *Dark City* (1998).

Hitler and Goebbels loved *Metropolis* and, after seeing the film, invited Lang to take charge of the Nationalist Socialist Cinema. Lang left for Paris the very same evening and from there went on to the USA where he continued his career in film until the 1960s.

Metropolis (1926)
German 55 × 38 in. (140 × 97 cm)
Courtesy of the Austrian National Library

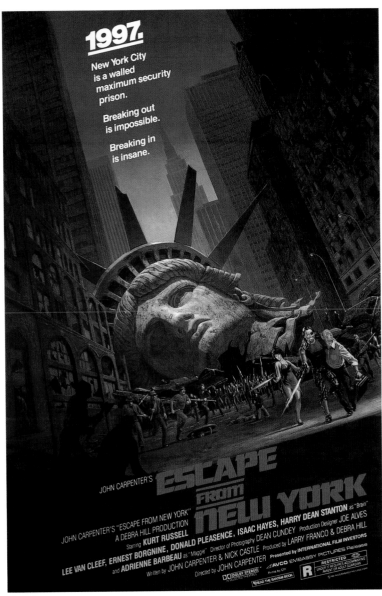

Escape From New York (1981)
US 41 × 27 in. (104 × 69 cm)
Illustration by Barry Jackson
Art direction by David Reneric
Courtesy of The Reel Poster Gallery

Escape From New York (1981)
US 41 × 27 in. (104 × 69 cm)
(Advance)
Art by S. Watts
Courtesy of The Reel Poster Gallery

Wieslaw Walkuski (b. 1956) studied at the Warsaw Academy of Fine Arts in the late seventies before beginning work as a poster designer for Pol Film and Film Polski, two of Poland's largest film distributors. He has worked for several publishing houses and theatres and has been freelance since 1987. He has won numerous accolades for his striking poster designs, of which *Escape From New York* is a powerful example. It is interesting that, like Walkuski, the two designers of the American posters for the film chose the Statue of Liberty as a symbol. Its destruction is a powerful metaphor for the collapse of order and freedom in New York, where the film is set.

Escape From New York (Ucieczka Z Nowego Jorku) (1981)
Polish 37 × 26 in. (94 × 66 cm)
Art by Wieslaw Walkuski
Courtesy of The Reel Poster Gallery

実験的
芸術的
冒険的"半SF"
＝ジャン＝リュック・ゴダール＝

1965年ベルリン映画祭
グランプリ受賞

ALPHAVILLE

エデイ・コンスタンチーヌ／アンナ・カリーナ／エイキム・タミロフ／ハワード・ヴェルノン／クリスタ・ラング
監督・脚本・脚色・台詞■ジャン＝リュック・ゴダール＝
撮影■ラウル・クタール／録音■ルネ・ルヴェール／音楽■ポール・ミスラキ
日本Ａ・Ｔ・Ｇ配給 仏・伊合作映画

Alphaville, Une Étrange Aventure De Lemmy Caution (1965)
Japanese 30 × 20 in. (76 × 51 cm)
Art by Noriroku Higaki
Courtesy of The Nouvelle Vague Collection

Alphaville is an unorthodox and ambitious science fiction film by the noted French New Wave director, Jean-Luc Godard. A stylized mélange of the hypnotic and the bizarre, the film challenges the very concept of science fiction as it moves effortlessly across a whole range of genres, including black comedy. The film is very noir in feel and indeed Lemmy Caution, the hero, is a detective in French adventure stories. The French poster by **Jean Mascii** (b. 1926) captures this blend of genres perfectly and is one of the artist's most famous designs.

Alphaville shares none of the characteristics common to science fiction: the world of the future looks remarkably similar to 1960s Paris where the film was, in fact, shot. However, *Alphaville* does borrow from *1984* and Huxley's *Brave New World*; Caution is on a mission to destroy Alpha 60, the computer that controls the population and that has outlawed emotion. Those who indulge in poetry and love are condemned to death, and one of the most surreal scenes in the film shows capital punishment being incorporated into a synchronized swimming event. The influence of *Alphaville* is evident in both Kubrick's *2001: A Space Odyssey* (1968) and Ridley Scott's *Blade Runner* (1982).

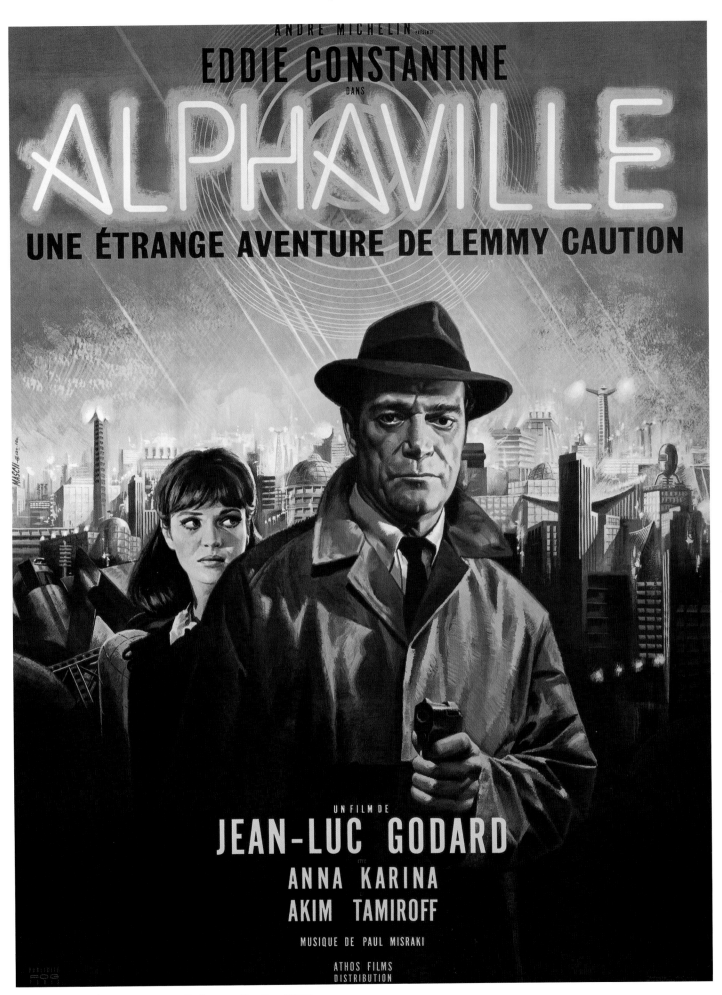

Alphaville, Une Étrange Aventure De Lemmy Caution (1965)
French 63 × 47 in. (160 × 119 cm)
Art by Jean Mascii
Courtesy of The Nouvelle Vague Collection

Total Recall (1990)
US 41 × 27 in. (104 × 69 cm)
(Advance)
Illustration by Mark Westermoe
Design by Clive Baillie
Art direction by Tom Seiniger and Mike Kaiser
Courtesy of The Reel Poster Gallery

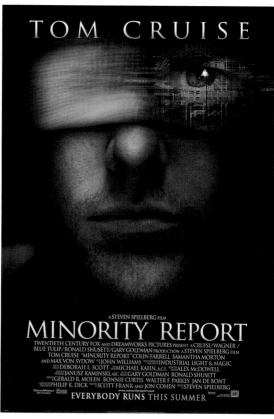

Minority Report (2002)
US 41 × 27 in. (104 × 69 cm)
(Advance)

The legacy of **Philip K. Dick** (1938–1982) boasts thirty-six novels and five short story collections. Regarded as one of the most intelligent science fiction writers of the twentieth century, Dick's writings question and analyze the very nature of our existence and our conception of the universe. His stories are set in complex and convoluted worlds where all perceptions are misleading and reality is seldom what it seems. His labyrinthine plots reflect Dick's own deeply troubled life, which was punctuated by a series of psychological crises.

He often questions the moral and ethical implications of technological advancement, a theme very evident in *Blade Runner*, based on his 1968 novel, *Do Androids Dream Of Electric Sheep?* Although very different in style and interpretation, the same motifs of paranoia, mistrust and unease can by found in both *Total Recall*, which was based on the short story *We Can Remember It For You Wholesale*, and in *Minority Report*, again based on one of Dick's short stories. The work of this most visionary of science fiction writers has influenced a stream of other films, most notably *The Matrix* (1999).

John Alvin (b. 1948) has been working as an illustrator for over twenty-five years and is most famous for his posters promoting fantasy, animation and science fiction films. Over the past quarter-century, he has produced the key art for more than 125 campaigns. After studying advertising, design and illustration, Alvin moved west and quickly found work in Hollywood. His career in poster design began at a time when big studios were closing down and advertising campaigns were no longer handled by the studios' publicity departments; his ability to obtain commissions when there was little demand for the work of poster artists is a testament to his unique talent. His posters are created in the traditional way; they are the product of an individual vision implemented with a high degree of technical skill. This is in marked contrast to present day practice, where a single piece of film poster imagery is the product of many different hands – those of an art director, a graphic designer and a computer animator, to name but a few. Alvin's individualistic style can be clearly identified in the poster for *Blade Runner*, which gained him widespread recognition as a master artist in the field.

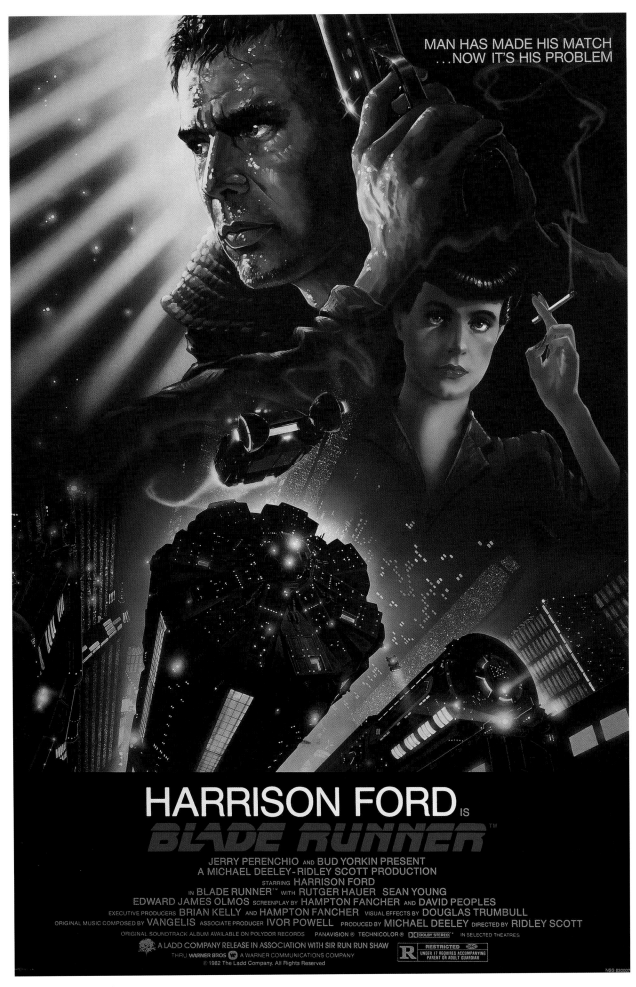

Blade Runner (1982)
US 41 × 27 in. (104 × 69 cm)
Art by John Alvin
Courtesy of The Reel Poster Gallery

THX 1138 (1971)
British 30 × 40 in. (76 × 102 cm)
Courtesy of the James Lavelle Collection

1984 (1956)
US 41 × 27 in. (104 × 69 cm)

Science fiction is the world of the alternative; an alternative universe, an alternative past or an alternative future. While these visions do include the utopian paradise, the future is more often bleakly dystopian and warns of the dark underworld of humanity's advancement. The horrors that are seen lying in wait for us are often extrapolations of the problems that beset our own world – the oppression of tyrannical regimes or the pressures to conform that restrict individuals even within 'free' societies. *THX 1138* and *1984* both envisage a deeply depressing future in which a ruling elite rigidly controls the population. Writing in 1948, George Orwell painted a picture of a Britain ruled by a Soviet-style regime presided over by the omnipresent 'Big Brother'. Although his book was banned in communist Russia, top Soviet officials are alleged to have used it as a handbook that offered useful tips on subjugating a population. The same sense of suffocation is conveyed in Woody Allen's *Sleeper*, but with a lighter touch. Although much of the story is played for laughs, we are again offered the prospect of a future in which the pressures to conform will be relentless.

As well as estimating political and social trends, science fiction is fond of extending existing scientific and technological developments into the future. Thus, in 1970, when *Sleeper* was made, cloning was still only a hypothetical possibility. Yet it was only twenty-three years later that Dolly the Sheep, the first cloned mammal, was born in Scotland. *Sleeper* also touches on the science of cryogenics. After dying in the 1970s, Woody Allen is frozen and unwrapped 200 years in the future. Today, the ability to resuscitate deep-frozen corpses still eludes us, but such is the faith in the inevitable progress of science that growing numbers of people are already spending ever-increasing amounts of money on having their bodies frozen after death. Andy Warhol and Walt Disney are amongst those waiting to be reborn.

Sleeper (1974)
US 41 × 27 in. (104 × 69 cm)
Courtesy of the Andy Johnson Collection

Ray Bradbury's *Fahrenheit 451* is set in a dystopian future where all books are forbidden and, if discovered, burned. The original version of this story was printed in a popular science fiction magazine in 1953 at the height of McCarthyite hysteria. Many writers and artists were being targeted in the senator's witch-hunt and censorship was rife. Bradbury's article was later expanded into a novel and then adapted for the screen in 1966. It is a lasting comment about the ignorance and brutality that results from a lack of education.

Fahrenheit 451 (1966)
French 63 × 47 in. (160 × 119 cm)
Art by Guy Gerard Noël
Courtesy of The Nouvelle Vague Collection

Fahrenheit 451 (1966)
Japanese 30 × 20 in. (76 × 51 cm)
Art by Shunji Sakai
Courtesy of The Nouvelle Vague Collection

Houston bikers execute a defensive move against a Tokyo Rollerball power play.

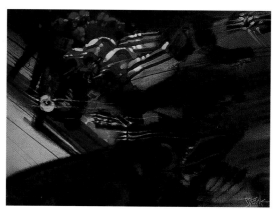

New York Transportation Corporation skaters oppose Houston Energy in the final Rollerball playoff game.

A London Communication Corporation scoring play against Houston in the Rollerball playoffs.

The Houston defense hitting a Paris Rollerball carrier in an Intercorporation playoff game.

An action highlight from the Tokyo Luxury Corporation Rollerball playoffs against London.

A New York Rollerball skater is taken out of the play by Madrid Food Corporation bikers.

Rollerball (1975)
US 17 × 19 in. (43 × 48 cm)
(Set of six Special Displays)
Art by Bob Peak
Courtesy of The Reel Poster Gallery

The studded glove image employed by Bob Peak for the *Rollerball* campaign proved so vivid and powerful that the concept was adopted for the majority of international campaigns for the film. Peak also designed a set of unique special display posters that were handed out in a deluxe, silver packet to the studio executives at the film's premiere. Painted on location, they depict the film's most memorable sequences and beautifully illustrate the deadly pace and speed of *Rollerball*.

Bob Peak (1927–1992) was born in Denver, Colorado and studied at The Art Center College of Design in Los Angeles. He was one of the most prolific and highly respected illustrators and painters of his generation, commanding record-breaking fees for his work, which ranged from designs for postage stamps through to fine art. His portfolio includes over forty-five covers of *Time* magazine and over one hundred film posters. Often described as the 'father of the modern movie poster', Peak developed a whole new approach to the art-form, abandoning the traditional use of collage and photomontage of the stars in favour of striking and original artwork. His style is characterized by a fantastic use of shadow and light and by candy-coloured, expressionistic backgrounds. Peak received many accolades in the course of his career and was inducted into the Illustrator's Hall of Fame in 1977. Aside from *Rollerball*, his other work in the science fiction genre includes *Superman The Movie* (1978) and the *Star Trek* series of films.

Rollerball (1975)
US 22 × 17 in. (56 × 43 cm)
Original Artwork. Pastel on board. Signed lower right.
Art by Bob Peak
Courtesy of The Reel Poster Gallery

Being the adventures of a young man whose principal interests are rape, ultra-violence and Beethoven.

STANLEY KUBRICK'S

CLOCKWORK ORANGE 'X'

A Stanley Kubrick Production "A CLOCKWORK ORANGE" Starring Malcolm McDowell
Patrick Magee · Adrienne Corri and Miriam Karlin · Screenplay by Stanley Kubrick
Based on the novel by Anthony Burgess · Produced and Directed by Stanley Kubrick
Executive Producers Max L. Raab and Si Litvinoff · From Warner Bros., A Kinney Company
Released by Columbia-Warner Distributors Ltd · Original Soundtrack recording on Warner Bros. K46127.

A Clockwork Orange (1971)
British 30 × 40 in. (76 × 102 cm)
Art by Philip Castle
Creative direction by Mike Kaplan
Courtesy of The Reel Poster Gallery

Philip Castle was born in Britain in 1942. After graduating from the Huddersfield School of Art, he obtained an MA from the Royal College of Art in 1967. Castle has had an interesting and diverse career. He was responsible for the famous Heineken Beer campaign in 1975 that featured *Star Trek*'s Spock; he has designed album covers for several pop groups, including *Pulp*; he has designed a number of film posters, including *Mars Attacks!* (see p. 104) and he worked with Allen Jones (b. 1937) on the legendary *Pirelli* calendars in the seventies. His most recent commission is an advertising campaign for Reebok. His instantly recognizable style is characterized by a unique airbrushing technique.

Philip Castle's artwork was used on posters for *A Clockwork Orange* across the world, each country altering the design only slightly, if at all. On the German, Danish and Argentinian posters, the sculpted figure is naked, but she was covered up for the rest of the world. David Pelham's contrasting design was originally used on the paperback tie-in book for the film in Canada. Kubrick liked the idea of using this design for the R-rated, slightly tamer version of the film, which was released soon after the X-rated version. A test run was printed but Kubrick's decision was overturned and Castle's artwork was again used on the R-rated poster.

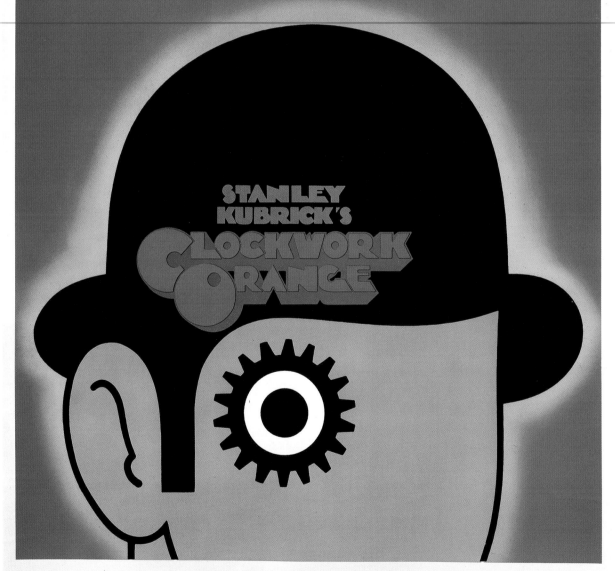

A Clockwork Orange (1971)
US 41 × 27 in. (104 × 69 cm)
(R-rated – Withdrawn)
Art by David Pelham
Courtesy of the James Lavelle Collection

The War Game (1967)
British 30 × 40 in. (76 × 102 cm)
Art by Romek Marber
Courtesy of The Reel Poster Gallery

Overnight, Hiroshima revealed the horrifying reality of nuclear weapons and made it plain that humanity had finally acquired the knowledge that could lead to its own annihilation. The BBC's *The War Game* is a bleak and disturbing docu-drama about the effects of nuclear war on an English city. The hand-held footage and documentary approach give the film a harrowing realism. Considered too controversial and shocking for the BBC when first produced, the film was instead given a limited theatrical showing and won an Oscar for Best Documentary in 1967.

Tomi Ungerer (b. 1931) is one of the most important satiric artists of the twentieth century. Born in France, he moved to the States in 1956 and began working for *The New York Times*. By 1958, he was drawing cartoons for *New Yorker*, *Esquire*, *Fortune* and *Harpers* to name but a few. Many of his best-known drawings are represented in *The Underground Sketchbook* (1964), a sardonic reflection on the habits of his contemporaries. He is famous for his anti-Vietnam War posters, which have sold worldwide, and he is the author of several illustrated works. Ungerer himself estimates that he has produced between 30,000 and 40,000 drawings over the course of forty years.

Peter Sellers • George C. Scott

in Stanley Kubrick's

Dr. Strangelove

Or:
How
I Learned
To
Stop
Worrying
And
Love
The
Bomb

the hot-line suspense comedy

also starring **Sterling Hayden · Keenan Wynn · Slim Pickens** and introducing Tracy Reed (as "Miss Foreign Affairs")
Screenplay by **Stanley Kubrick, Peter George & Terry Southern** Based on the book "Red Alert" by Peter George
Produced & Directed by **Stanley Kubrick** · A Columbia Pictures Release

Dr. Strangelove (1964)
US 41 × 27 in. (104 × 69 cm)
Art by Tomi Ungerer
Courtesy of The Reel Poster Gallery

28 Days Later (2002)
British 60 × 40 in. (152 × 102 cm)
(Advance)
Illustration by Glyn Dillon
Design by Andrew Nicholau – Creative Partnership
Courtesy of the Andrew MacDonald Collection

In Danny Boyle's *28 Days Later*, Britain has been devastated by a plague that turns people into raging zombies and only a handful of survivors remain. Although a fantasy, the film is a chilling reminder of humanity's vulnerability to a simple infection.

Glyn Dillon's artwork for the British advance 60 × 40 inch poster was also used in an effective campaign in the London Underground where a series of posters were seen in sequence as passengers rode up or down an escalator.

On The Beach was released simultaneously in twelve countries around the world. Each country had one of their top illustrators design a poster for the film. Italian artist Nicola Simbari's design proved so interesting that United Artists decided to use it on an alternative style American one-sheet poster.

● **1914.** H. G. Wells predicts atomic bombs in his novel *The World Set Free*.
● **1945, 6 August.** The first atomic bomb ever to be used in war, *Little Boy*, devastates Hiroshima. Three days later, *Fat Man* is dropped on Nagasaki. Thousands are killed and thousands more die from radiation in the years that follow.

On The Beach (1959)
US 41 × 27 in. (104 × 69 cm)
(Style B)
Art by Nicola Simbari
Courtesy of the Andrew MacDonald Collection

Unlike many of the relatively light-hearted science-fiction films of the fifties, *The Quatermass Xperiment* is a genuinely frightening film made with serious intent and was given an X certificate by the British censors. (The title was adapted to exploit the certification.) The combination of menace and paranoia that marked Quatermass out from its contemporaries proved a successful mix, and there were three sequels: *Quatermass II* (1957), *Quatermass and the Pit* (1967) and *The Quatermass Conclusion* (1979). The film was also the inspiration for the nineties science fiction series *The X-Files*.

The Quatermass Xperiment (Zemsta Kosmosu) (1955)
Polish 33 × 23 in. (84 × 58 cm)
Art by Marian Stachurski
Courtesy of The Reel Poster Gallery

Marian Stachurski (1931–1980) graduated from the Warsaw Academy of Art in 1956. Her poster for *The Quatermass Xperiment* is a perfect example of her style, which combines graphic design and abstract illustration. In contrast, Clement Hurel's design for the French poster for *Quatermass II* features a dreamlike, haunting image that reflects the tense menace of the film.

Quatermass II: Enemy From Space (Terre Contre Satellite) (1957)
French 63 × 47 in. (160 × 119 cm)
Art by Clement Hurel
Courtesy of The Reel Poster Gallery

Set in a post-apocalyptic outback, the Australian-made *Mad Max* propelled Mel Gibson to international stardom. The movie features some of the best road stunts ever filmed and spawned two sequels. The tagline used on the Australian poster was later adapted for international use.

Mad Max (1979)
British 41 × 27 in. (104 × 69 cm)
(International)
Art by Hamagami
Courtesy of the Andy Johnson Collection

Mad Max (1979)
Australian 40 × 27 in. (102 × 69 cm)
Courtesy of the Steve & Kanella Wilson Collection

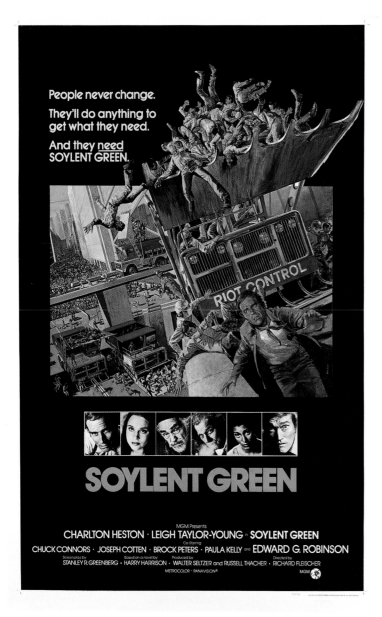

Soylent Green (1973)
US 41 × 27 in. (104 × 69 cm)
Art by John Solie
Courtesy of The Reel Poster Gallery

Silent Running (1971)
US 41 × 27 in. (104 × 69 cm)
Courtesy of the Andy Johnson Collection

A number of the science-fiction films of the early seventies were inspired by the perceived threats of moral and/or environmental decay and warned against the dangers they posed to the future of mankind. *Soylent Green* and *Silent Running* are eco-films that challenge our ruthless pursuit of progress at the expense of the environment. *Logan's Run*, on the other hand, is a backlash against the fascination with youth in the sixties and seventies that led people to treat the older generation as dispensable.

Logan's Run (1976)
US 41 × 27 in. (104 × 69 cm)
(Advance)
Courtesy of the Andy Johnson Collection

Daikaij Gamera (Gammera The Invincible) (1965)
Japanese 60 × 20 in. (152 × 51 cm)
Courtesy of the Helmut Hamm Collection

Ghidra: The Three-Headed Monster (1956)
Japanese 30 × 20 in. (76 × 51 cm)
Courtesy of the Helmut Hamm Collection

Godzilla, King of the Monsters created a whole new sub-genre of science fiction, spawning numerous sequels and inspiring a stream of giant-reptile flicks that continues to this day. Originally released in Japan in 1954 as *Gojira*, several scenes were added for the American release two years later, with Raymond Burr playing reporter Steve Martin. A dinosaur from the Jurassic era, Godzilla is brought back to life because of underwater nuclear tests. The creature's killing rampage in Tokyo charges the original with a serious anti-nuclear message. This ominous tone was to change in many of the sequels, where Godzilla acquires a friendlier disposition.

Godzilla, King Of The Monsters (1956)
US 60 × 40 in. (152 × 102 cm)
Courtesy of The Reel Poster Gallery

The Lost World (1925)
US 16 × 14 in. (41 × 36 cm) (trimmed)

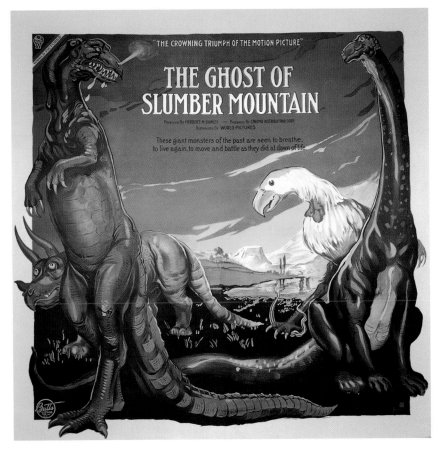

The Ghost Of Slumber Mountain (1918)
US 81 × 81 in. (206 × 206 cm)
Art by Potter
Courtesy of The Reel Poster Gallery

From Tyrannosaurus Rex to the Loch Ness Monster, dinosaurs have exerted a powerful hold over the human imagination ever since palaeontologists first revealed that the Earth had once been populated by giant reptiles. Two early films, *The Ghost of Slumber Mountain* and *The Lost World*, exploited such interest. The latter was based upon the premise that surviving populations of dinosaurs might yet be discovered in remote parts of the world; an idea that was then neglected for several decades until Steven Spielberg gave it a new twist in his 1993 blockbuster *Jurassic Park*.

The Ghost of Slumber Mountain was the first feature-length film to make use of the stop-motion special effects developed by maestro of the art **Willis O'Brien** (1886–1962). Originally a newspaper cartoonist and cowboy, O'Brien developed the stop-motion technique in 1914; *The Ghost Of Slumber Mountain* was his first major project, followed by the *The Lost World* in 1925. His reputation attained legendary status in 1933 with the release of *King Kong* and he continued his illustrious career into the sixties. His other films include *Mighty Joe Young* (1949), which won an Oscar for its special effects, and the 1960 remake of *The Lost World*.

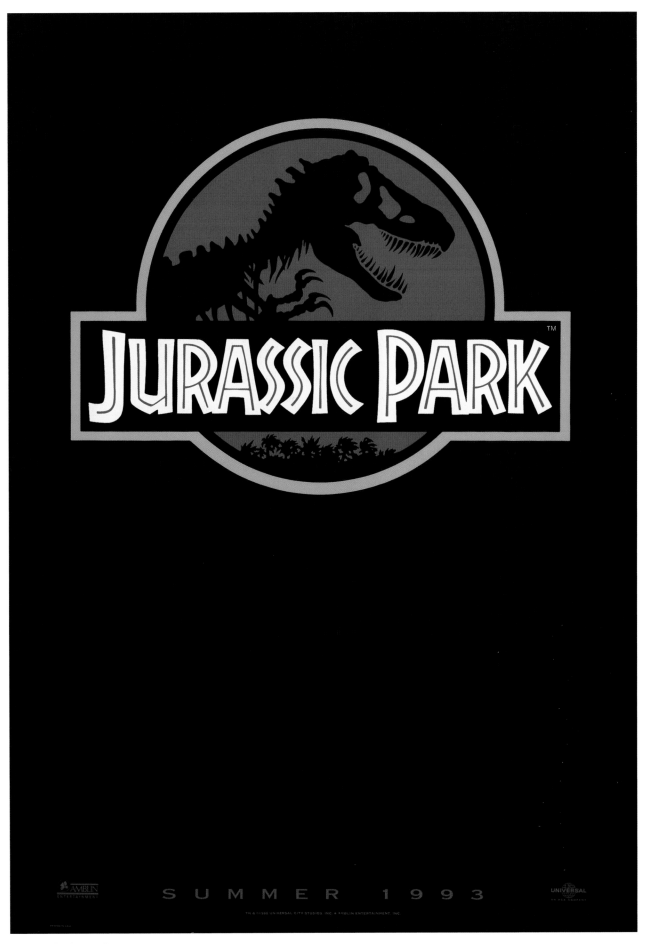

Jurassic Park (1993)
US 41 × 27 in. (104 × 69 cm)
(Advance)
Art by Chip Kidd
Art direction and design by Tom Martin
Creative direction by David Sameth
Courtesy of the Martin Bridgewater Collection

Tarantula (1955)
US 41 × 27 in. (104 × 69 cm)
Art by Reynold Brown
Courtesy of the Helmut Hamm Collection

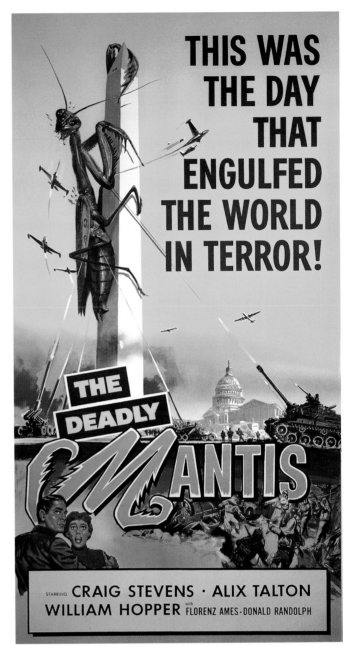

The Deadly Mantis (1957)
US 81 × 41 in. (206 × 104 cm)
Art by Reynold Brown

Monsters are not confined to the realm of the horror flick. Numerous giant ants, wasp women and killer tarantulas roam the science fiction films of the 1950s. Such creations gained a new scientific 'respectability' after the discovery of the structure of DNA made the mutant a more credible scientific possibility, encouraging the idea that there was a real threat of existing species being altered by scientific experiments or nuclear radiation.

● **1953**. James Watson and Francis Crick solve the structure of DNA and reveal the double helix.

Them (Assalto Alla Terra) (1954)
Italian 55 × 39 in. (140 × 99 cm)
Art by Luigi Martinati
Courtesy of the Richard and Barbara Allen Collection

The Fly (1958)
British 30 × 40 in. (76 × 102 cm)
Art by 'Jock' Hinchcliff
Courtesy of The Reel Poster Gallery

The Fly is a perfect example of an entity that became part of the science-fiction repertoire after Crick and Watson's discovery of the double helix – the DNA mutant. The poster, which challenged the audience to 'prove it didn't happen', played on public anxiety about the implications of the discovery while also offering the titillating prospect of seeing man-made monsters on-screen. The central character, Andre Delambre, is a scientist who, while experimenting with his 'matter transporter', accidentally mixes his own DNA with that of a fly. Two creatures result: a man with the head and leg of a fly, and a fly with the head and arm of a man. Andre's wife, Helene, soon learns of the horrendous blunder and is faced with the moral dilemma of whether to end her husband's life. The finale of the film is vividly captured in 'Jock' Hinchcliff's kitsch poster.

The Wasp Woman (1960)
US 41 × 27 in. (104 × 69 cm)
Courtesy of the Helmut Hamm Collection

People have always been fascinated by the sea and the secrets that may lurk in its depths; even today the ocean depths are one of the few regions on our planet that remain unexplored. Throughout history, sailors have reported encounters with giant serpents, squid or other mysterious sea creatures and over the centuries many vessels have disappeared in strange and sinister circumstances. No wonder, then, that science fiction has frequently ventured beneath the waves and sought to exploit the various myths and legends of the sea, from Atlantis to the Bermuda Triangle. *It Came From Beneath The Sea* is a perfect example of this genre, as is *The Abyss.* The latter film is set deep underwater where the crew of a submersible encounter an alien presence. Although many different posters for the film were produced around the world, the East German design is the only one that attempts to depict the alien creature, albeit an artistic interpretation of the entity.

It Came From Beneath The Sea (Il Mostro Dei Mari) (1955)
Italian 55 × 39 in. (140 × 99 cm)
Art by Alfredo Capitani

The Abyss (Abyss) (1989)
East German 33 × 23 in. (84 × 58 cm)
Courtesy of The Reel Poster Gallery

Originally filmed in 3D, *Creature From The Black Lagoon* is a hybrid of science fiction and horror. A fossil-hunting expedition ventures deep into the heart of the Amazon jungle and encounters 'gill-man', a monster that lives in the murky depths of a lagoon. The film proved a success and the creature returned from the mists to star in two sequels, *Revenge Of The Creature* (1955) and *The Creature Walks Among Us* (1956).

Creature From The Black Lagoon (1954)
US 41 × 27 in. (104 × 69 cm)
Art by Reynold Brown
Courtesy of The Reel Poster Gallery

Creature From The Black Lagoon (Der Schrecken Vom Amazonas) (1954)
German 33 × 23 in. (84 × 58 cm)
Art by Bruno Rehak
Courtesy of the Helmut Hamm Collection

The Creature Walks Among Us (1956)
US 81 × 41 in. (206 × 104 cm)
Art by Reynold Brown
Courtesy of The Reel Poster Gallery

Revenge Of The Creature (1955)
US 81 × 41 in. (206 × 104 cm)
Art by Reynold Brown

Reynold Brown (1917–1991) won a scholarship to attend art school in the early thirties. He embarked on a career in comic book art until a providential meeting with Norman Rockwell convinced him to pursue his dream of becoming an illustrator. Moving to New York at the end of the Second World War, Brown started designing covers for magazines and books, including *Popular Science* and the paperback editions of the *Perry Mason* mysteries.

Brown moved into designing movie posters through Universal Studios. His career spanned over 250 campaigns between 1952 and 1970 and included artwork for *Ben Hur* (1959), *Spartacus* (1960), *The Alamo* (1960) and *Dr. Zhivago* (1965). He is most renowned for his work in science fiction and horror 'B' movies, including *The Incredible Shrinking Man* (1957) and *Attack Of The 50 Foot Woman* (1958). He had a gift for creating detailed scenes of epic grandeur and mass panic that fittingly reflect the suspicion and paranoia of the age. Brown also taught at the Art Center College of Design, where two of his students were illustrators Bob Peak and Drew Struzan. (See pp. 30 and 142.)

Creature From The Black Lagoon (1954)
US 81 × 41 in. (206 × 104 cm)
Art by Reynold Brown
Courtesy of the Andrew Cohen Collection

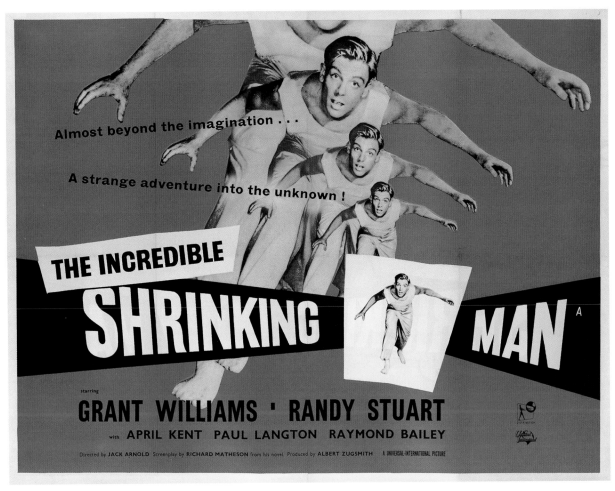

The Incredible Shrinking Man (1957)
British 30 × 40 in. (76 × 102 cm)
Courtesy of the Helmut Hamm Collection

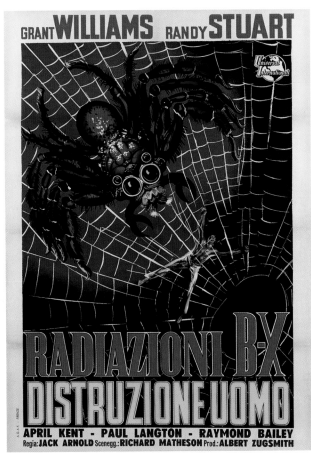

**The Incredible Shrinking Man
(Radiazioni B X Distruzione Uomo)** (1957)
Italian 55 × 39 in. (140 × 99 cm)
Courtesy of The Reel Poster Gallery

Size is a common theme in the 'What if…?' world of science fiction and the genre has often explored scenarios in which the scale of the everyday world becomes distorted. *The Incredible Shrinking Man* is a great example of this sub-genre. Whilst sunbathing one day, Scott Carey is enveloped by a mysterious cloud and shortly afterwards starts to shrink at an alarming rate. By the end of the film, Carey is little bigger than a dust particle; he has lost his family, his friends and has become prey for the common house spider. He summarizes his new existence with the concluding line, 'Smaller than smallest, I meant something too. To God there is no zero. I still exist!' The film resists the temptation to become a simple piece of science fiction/horror and is instead an existential exploration of the deep psychological effects on Carey of his changing scale. Reynold Brown was responsible for the American poster campaign for the film and his artwork is considered to be among the classics of the genre.

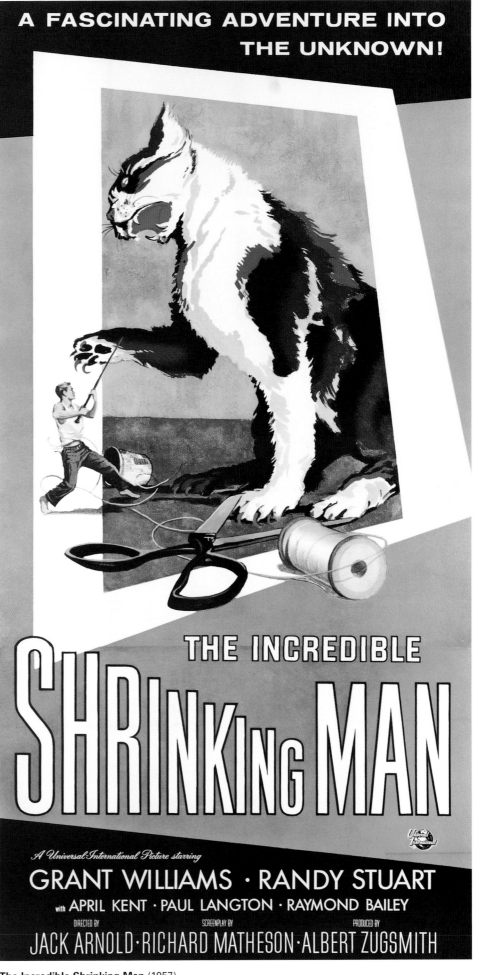

The Incredible Shrinking Man (1957)
US 81 × 41 in. (206 × 104 cm)
Art by Reynold Brown
Courtesy of the Andy Johnson Collection

Doctor Cyclops (Dr. Cyclops) (1940)
Italian 79 × 55 in. (201 × 140 cm)
Art by Carlantonio Longi

Attack Of The 50 Foot Woman is an unashamedly second-rate, science fiction B-movie. Nevertheless, Reynold Brown's American poster for the film, depicting an outsized Allison Hayes, magnificently proportioned and minimally clad, is considered a masterpiece that has, ironically, become more famous than the film itself.

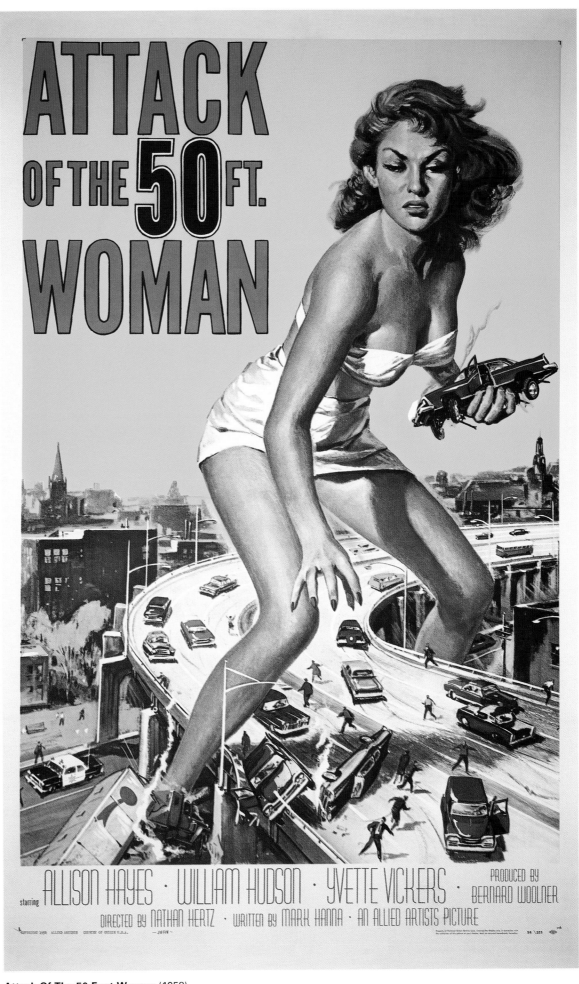

Attack Of The 50 Foot Woman (1958)
US 41 × 27 in. (104 × 69 cm)
Art by Reynold Brown
Courtesy of the Helmut Hamm Collection

The Blob (Fluido Mortale) (1958)
Italian 79 × 55 in. (201 × 140 cm)
Art by Sandro Simeoni
Courtesy of The Haldane Collection

The Blob is a beautifully simple film. Although in many ways the archetypal teen-monster flick of the fifties, it has a distinct charm and a refreshingly un-Hollywood air to it. Directed by Irvin S. Yeaworth Jr. on a tight budget, the film is a little rough around the edges. However, the title credits are mindblowing and feature a soundtrack by Burt Bacharach and Mack David. These details combine to give *The Blob* a kitsch and lasting appeal.

The blob itself lands on Earth from a distant planet and the beginning of the film is creepily ominous as an old man becomes its first victim. A doctor is next to be absorbed by the pulsating mass and only Steve (also the name of McQueen's character) and his teenage friends seem aware of what is happening. Battling against the scepticism of the police, they finally convince the authorities to take action when the creature attacks the local movie theatre. In the final sequence the blob is frozen in a block of ice and dropped at the North Pole, only to be defrosted in 1972 for the sequel, *Beware The Blob*.

It Came From Outer Space is in many ways similar to *The Blob*; again, it features an alien life-form that crash lands on Earth and starts a panic in a small town. Joseph Smith's poster for the film is everything you could hope for in a fifties science fiction 3-D poster. In contrasting style, Sandro Simeoni's poster for *The Blob* chooses to depict the monster's 'deadly fluid' (also a literal translation of the Italian title).

It Came From Outer Space (1953)
US 81 × 41 in. (206 × 104 cm)
Art by Joseph Smith
Courtesy of the Andy Johnson Collection

The She-Creature (1956)
US 41 × 27 in. (104 × 69 cm)
Art by Albert Kallis

The Astounding She Monster (1957)
US 41 × 27 in. (104 × 69 cm)
Art by Albert Kallis

Albert Kallis worked for American International Pictures on an impressive list of 'B'-movie posters. (In fact, his colourful and enticing designs were in some cases a good deal more impressive than the films they advertised.) Kallis' design for *The Astounding She Monster* is a gorgeous image of model and stripper Shirley Kilpatrick. Interestingly, the first time Kilpatrick wore her monster suit, her curvaceous figure caused the seams to burst open at the back. If you watch the film closely, you will find that she always exits without turning.

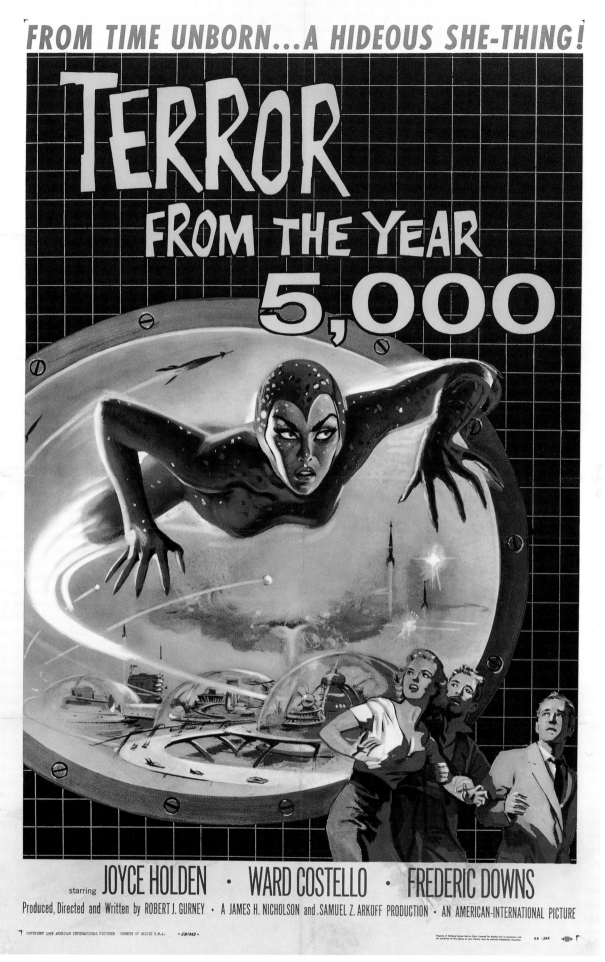

Terror From The Year 5000 (1958)
US 41 × 27 in. (104 × 69 cm)
Art by Albert Kallis
Courtesy of the Helmut Hamm Collection

Fantastic Voyage (1966)
Japanese 30 × 20 in. (76 × 51 cm)
Courtesy of The Reel Poster Gallery

Fantastic Voyage (Fantastická Cesta) (1966)
Czechoslovakian 33 × 23 in. (84 × 58 cm)
Courtesy of The Reel Poster Gallery

Both the titles and posters for *Fantastic Voyage* and *Innerspace* suggest routine science fiction settings in space or beneath the sea. In fact, both are set inside the human body. In *Fantastic Voyage* a scientist is on the verge of death and a medical team is miniaturized and injected into his body to locate and treat a blood clot. In order to complete its mission, the team has to navigate through cavernous bodily organs as well as overcoming an attempt at sabotage by one of the crew. The eighties comedy, *Innerspace*, has a similar premise that involves a Navy test pilot being accidentally injected into the body of a geeky store clerk.

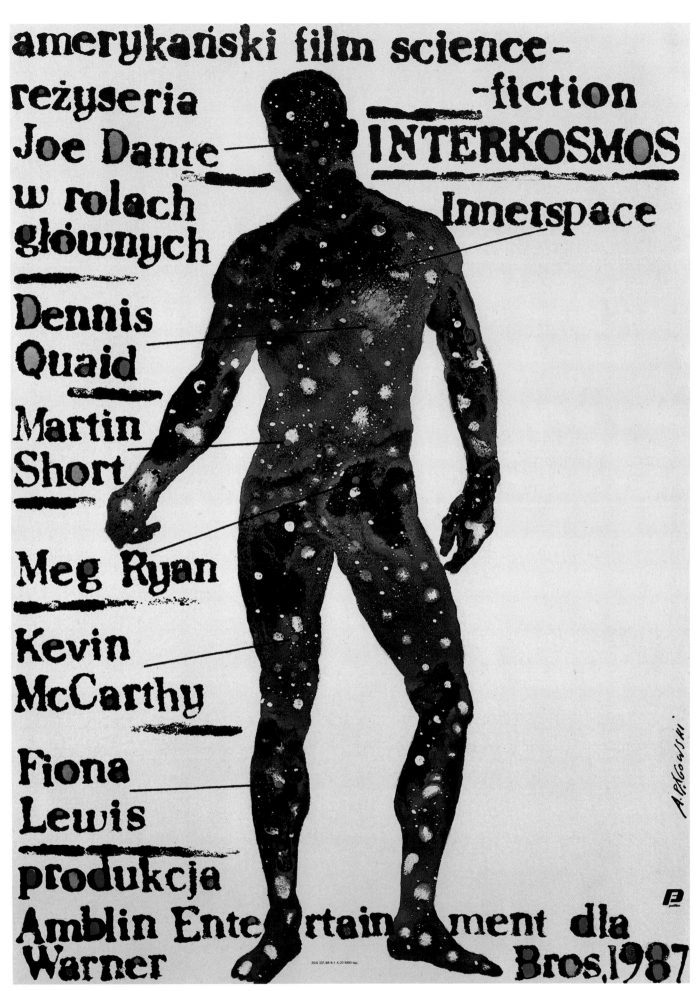

Innerspace (Interkosmos) (1987)
Polish 38 × 27 in. (97 × 69 cm)
Art by Andrzej Pagowski
Courtesy of The Reel Poster Gallery

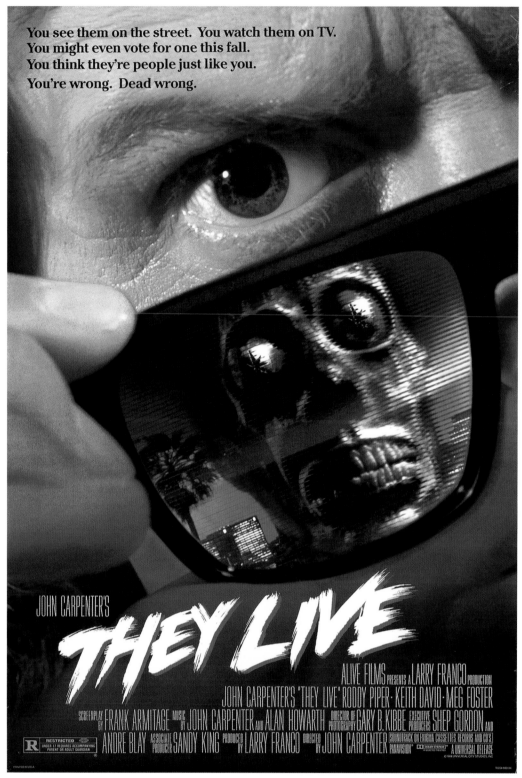

The science-fiction fable *X – The Man With The X-Ray Eyes* was directed by B-feature guru, Roger Corman. It follows the experiments of Dr Xavier, whose developments in vision allow him to see through walls and clothing, as demonstrated on the American poster for the film. Eventually, Xavier's powers of sight develop to such an extent that he can see into the depths of space and through the very fabric of reality itself.

They Live also explores perception and reality. John Nada is a drifter who discovers a pair of special sunglasses that allow him to see a startling reality in which the government is subjugating the population through subliminal messages and aliens have disguised themselves as Republicans (the film was, in part, a not very subtle satire on Reagan's America). Nada joins an underground resistance battling to eradicate the creatures.

They Live (1988)
US 41 × 27 in. (104 × 69 cm)
Design by David Reneric
Photo by Bruce McBroom
Art direction by Tom Martin
Courtesy of The Reel Poster Gallery

X – The Man With The X-Ray Eyes (1963)
US 41 × 27 in. (104 × 69 cm)
Courtesy of The Reel Poster Gallery

The Invisible Ray (1936)
US 41 × 27 in. (104 × 69 cm)
Art by Karoly Grosz
Courtesy of the Kirk Hammett Collection

Based on H. G. Wells' novel, *The Invisible Man* is both a horror and science fiction classic. It was the first film to juxtapose horrific and humorous elements and the director, James Whale, plays many of the scenes for laughs. The film gave Claude Rains his big break and he stars as 'The Invisible One', a scientist who, affected by side-effects from his experiments in visibility, is transformed into a murderous megalomaniac. The same theme is exploited in *The Invisible Ray*, where a well-intentioned scientist is searching for supplies of 'Radium X', an essential component for his new heat-ray. However, his overexposure to the element starts affecting his sanity and he is soon using his laser-like ray in demented attempts at murder.

The Invisible Man (1933)
US 41 × 27 in. (104 × 69 cm)
Art by Karoly Grosz
Courtesy of The Reel Poster Gallery

Mary Shelley (1797–1851) was only eighteen years old when she wrote *Frankenstein*, which has a good claim to be the first science fiction novel. The book remains a seminal classic and is a particularly interesting achievement for a female writer of the early nineteenth century. Although Shelley does not make it clear exactly how Frankenstein's monster is brought to life, electricity is certainly involved, and she had probably read about the work of the Italian, Luigi Galvani, who had recently demonstrated that the leg of a dissected frog would twitch when an electrical charge was applied to the nerve endings. Although *Frankenstein* has been adapted for the screen many times, Universal's 1931 production is still regarded as the definitive version of Shelley's classic.

Jacques Faria's artwork for the French poster is stylized and striking in its simplicity. Robert Florey, who was a significant contributor to the screenplay, is not credited on any poster for the film except the French one. Bruno Rehak's design for the German re-release is the only poster that depicts the legendary creation scene in the laboratory.

Frankenstein (1931)
German 33 × 23 in. (84 × 58 cm)
(Re-Release 1956)
Art by Bruno Rehak
Courtesy of The Reel Poster Gallery

Frankenstein (1931)
French 63 × 47 in. (160 × 119 cm)
(Style B)
Art by Jacques Faria
Courtesy of the Ian A. Nabeshima Collection

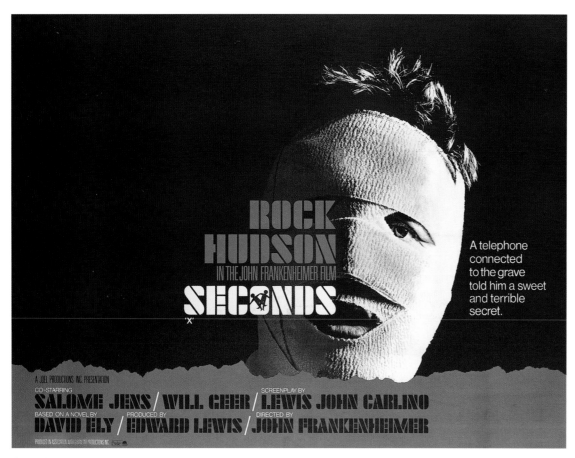

Seconds (1966)
British 30 × 40 in. (76 × 102 cm)
Courtesy of the Andy Johnson Collection

Seconds is an enigmatic and visceral film about identity and the superficial and unsatisfying quest for physical perfection and eternal youth. Arthur Hamilton is in his fifties, trapped in an insipid and monotonous existence, when he is offered the opportunity to change the whole course of his life by The Company, an elite team of plastic surgeons who can effectively replace an ageing body with one twenty years younger. Hamilton is now a 'second' and relocates to a hedonistic California for a second youth. However, he soon feels oppressed by the falsehood of his new existence and returns to The Company, only to discover the horrifying truth behind their experiments.

Saul Bass (1920–1996) studied at the Art Students League, graduated from Brooklyn College, and then, at the age of 26, moved West where he is credited with introducing an East Coast sensibility to marketing. He saw advertising as a means of funding his passion for the movies and, after six years working with a number of agencies, he finally had the funds to establish his own firm. All this time he was forging ever-closer links with the film industry and in 1954 this led to a commission from Otto Preminger to design the logo for the poster for *Carmen Jones*. Thus began an association with Preminger that would encompass another thirteen films, including *The Man With The Golden Arm* (1955) for which Bass would design the famous jagged limb. Bass also worked with a number of other respected directors, including Alfred Hitchcock, and made a number of films himself. His only other venture into science fiction was *Phase IV*, which he directed in 1974.

SECONDS

A JOHN FRANKENHEIMER FILM · ROCK HUDSON · SALOME JENS · WILL GEER · JOHN RANDOLPH · JEFF CORY
WESLEY ADDY · MURRAY HAMILTON · KARL SWENSON · KHIGH DHIGH · FRANCIS REID · RICHARD ANDERSON
SCREENPLAY BY LEWIS JOHN CARLINO · BASED ON A NOVEL BY DAVID ELY · MUSIC BY JERRY GOLDSMITH
PRODUCED BY EDWARD LEWIS · DIRECTED BY JOHN FRANKENHEIMER · A JOEL PRODUCTIONS RELEASE

Seconds (1966)
US 36 × 25 in. (91 × 64 cm)
(Unused Design)
Art by Saul Bass
Courtesy of the Tony Nourmand Collection

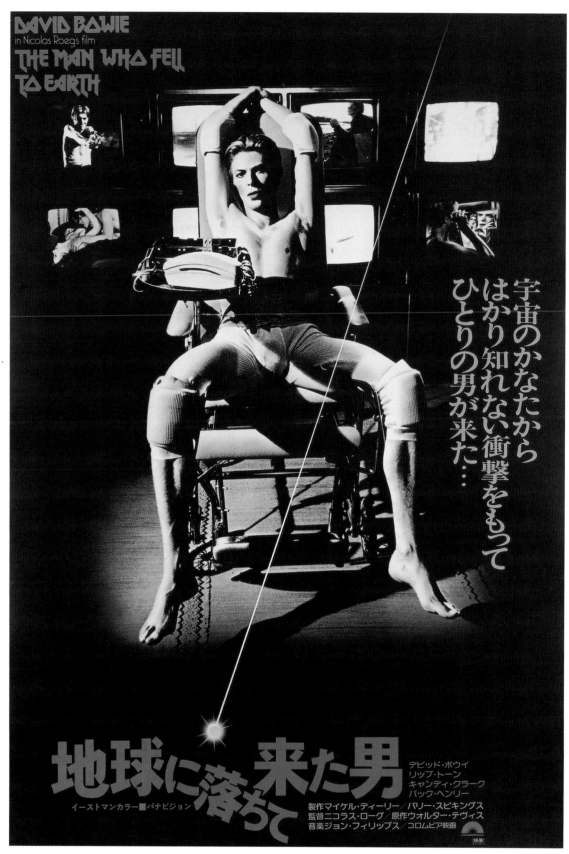

The Man Who Fell To Earth (1976)
Japanese 30 × 20 in. (76 × 51 cm)
Courtesy of the Robert Jess Roth Collection

Based on the novel by Walter Tevis, *The Man Who Fell To Earth* starred David Bowie, aka Ziggy Stardust, and was directed by Nicholas Roeg, whose work is noted for its strong visual sense acquired in his years as a cinematographer. Rich in symbolism, the film has an hallucinatory and stylized feel.

The Man Who Fell To Earth (1976)
British 20 × 20 in. (51 × 51 cm)
Original Artwork. Mixed media. Signed middle right.
Art by Vic Fair
Courtesy of The Reel Poster Gallery

**The Man Who Fell To Earth
(L' Uomo Che Cadde Sulla Terra)** (1976)
Italian 39 × 27 in. (99 × 69 cm)
(Style B)
Courtesy of The Reel Poster Gallery

**The Man Who Fell To Earth
(L' Uomo Che Cadde Sulla Terra)** (1976)
Italian 39 × 27 in. (99 × 69 cm)
(Style A)
Courtesy of The Reel Poster Gallery

Christian Simonpietri established his reputation as a photographer during the Vietnam War. In 1973 he co-founded the Sygma Photo Agency, where he continued to work as a photo-journalist covering other conflicts, including Bangladesh (1971), Chile (1973) and Nicaragua (1978). In the seventies he also began working as a still photographer on movie sets and in the music industry and has photographed a staggering list of stars. Simonpietri has stayed true to his journalistic roots, covering the Los Angeles riots in 1992, travelling to Kabul in 1996 and working as cameraman, producer and reporter for Sygma TV. The photograph on the American poster for *The Man Who Fell To Earth* was subsequently used for David Bowie's *Low* album.

The Man Who Fell To Earth (1976)
US 41 × 27 in. (104 × 69 cm)
Photo by Christian Simonpietri
Courtesy of The Reel Poster Gallery

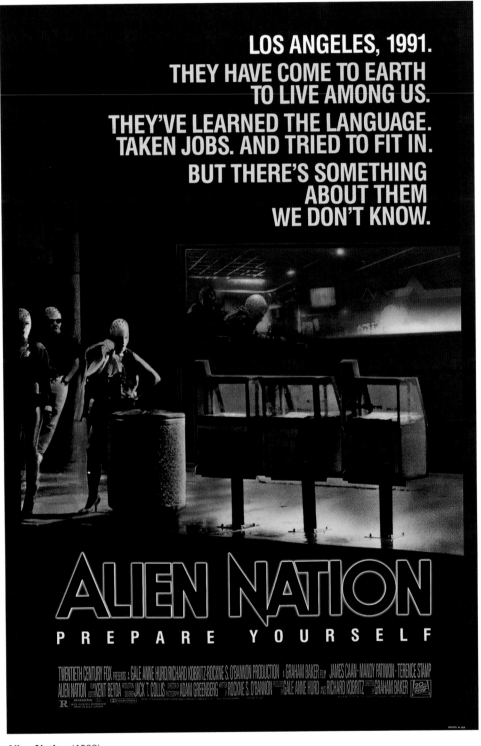

LOS ANGELES, 1991.
THEY HAVE COME TO EARTH
TO LIVE AMONG US.
THEY'VE LEARNED THE LANGUAGE.
TAKEN JOBS. AND TRIED TO FIT IN.
BUT THERE'S SOMETHING
ABOUT THEM
WE DON'T KNOW.

ALIEN NATION
P R E P A R E   Y O U R S E L F

Alien Nation and *The Brother From Another Planet* explore issues of racism and bigotry by examining the way in which a fictional society reacts to the appearance of an 'alien' presence. Science fiction often uses the camouflage of fantasy to disguise an examination of sensitive contemporary, social and political concerns. When topical hot potatoes are transplanted to a distant planet or an alternative universe, the audience is forced to set aside its prejudices and is freed to view the issues from a fresh perspective. The use of fantastical, or futuristic settings can also provide film-makers with a means of evading censorship and avoiding controversy.

Alien Nation (1988)
US 41 × 27 in. (104 × 69 cm)
Art direction and design by Henry Lehn
Photo by Jane O'Neal
Courtesy of The Reel Poster Gallery

STARRING JOE MORTON
PRODUCTION DESIGN NORA CHAVOOSHIAN
DIRECTOR OF PHOTOGRAPHY ERNEST R. DICKERSON
MUSIC BY MASON DARING
PRODUCED BY PEGGY RAJSKI AND MAGGIE RENZI
WRITTEN, DIRECTED AND EDITED BY JOHN SAYLES

The Brother From Another Planet (1984)
US 41 × 27 in. (104 × 69 cm)
(Style B)
Courtesy of Separate Cinema

Planet Of The Apes (Planeta Opic) (1968)
Czechoslovakian 33 × 23 in. (84 × 58 cm)
Courtesy of the Tomoaki 'Nigo' Nagao Collection

Planet Of The Apes (1968)
British 30 × 40 in. (76 × 102 cm)
Courtesy of The Reel Poster Gallery

Planet Of The Apes is based on the novel *La Planete Des Singes* (1963) by the French author Pierre Boulle. Its producers aimed to appeal to the imagination of younger viewers while still challenging adults with a subtle and timely commentary on social and political issues. Taylor, played by Charlton Heston, is one of a team of astronauts who land in what he considers to be an 'upside down world', where apes have evolved from man. This was the first time that apes were featured in a big budget film – previously their territory had been strictly confined to B-movies. *Planet Of The Apes* was hugely successful and was followed by no less than four sequels.

The film challenged people's assumptions about the nature of civilization and also, perhaps, aimed to question racial prejudice. Certainly when an American Afro-Caribbean audience watched one of the sequels, *Conquest Of The Planet Of The Apes* (1972), they cheered, as they believed that the film had truly demonstrated the brutality of slavery. Sadly, the film's social message is still as valid today.

The posters vary in design. Whereas the American and British campaigns feature more traditional artwork, many of the Eastern European countries, as is their wont, chose to depict the film in a more abstract style.

Planet Of The Apes (Planeta Maimutelor) (1968)
Romanian 38 × 27 in. (97 × 69 cm)
Courtesy of The Reel Poster Gallery

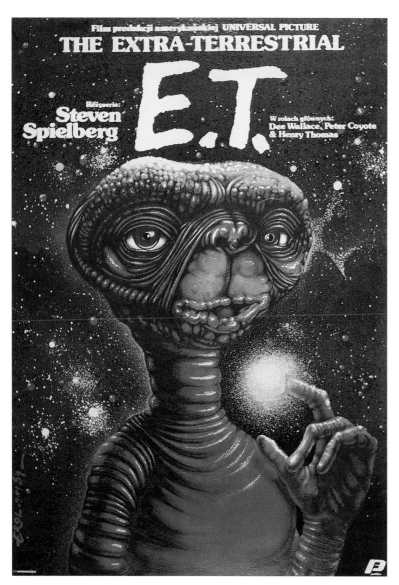

E.T. The Extra Terrestrial (1982)
Polish 36 × 27 in. (91 × 69 cm)
Art by Jakub Erol
Courtesy of The Reel Poster Gallery

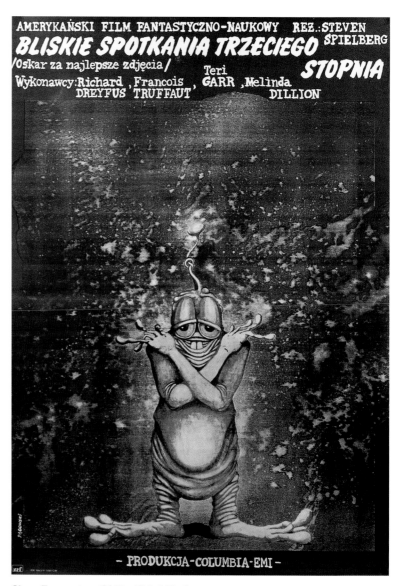

Close Encounters Of The Third Kind
(Bliskie Spotkania Trzeciego Stopnia) (1977)
Polish 38 × 27 in. (97 × 69 cm)
Art by Andrzej Pagowski
Courtesy of The Reel Poster Gallery

The Polish posters for *E.T. The Extra Terrestrial* and *Close Encounters Of The Third Kind* are markedly similar in style. Although Erol's *E.T.* is an accurate portrait of the creature in the film, amusingly, Pagowski's alien bears no resemblance to those in *Close Encounters*. Both artists have had extensive and successful careers. **Jakub Erol** (b. 1941) has concentrated on illustration work, posters and graphic art. He graduated from the Academy of Fine Arts in Warsaw in 1968 and was responsible for over 200 posters between 1966 and 1992. **Andrzej Pagowski** (b. 1953) graduated from Poznan College of Visual Art in 1978. He has twice won the Hollywood Reporter Key Art Award and exhibitions of his work have been mounted around the world.

Spielberg's *E.T.* encapsulates the magic of childhood. It is a poignant and bittersweet science fiction adventure about one boy's remarkable friendship with E.T., an alien accidentally abandoned on Earth. The boy, Elliott, must help E.T. return home to safety before he is captured by the cynical government or other self-interested adults. The scene with the bicycle flying past the moon is one of cinema's most enduring moments and the image was the basis for the Style A American poster. However, this design was never used because, allegedly, Spielberg did not want to reveal this image before the release of the film and also because the director wanted to use this as the logo for his company, *Amblin*. *E.T.* is an enduring family favourite that remains one of the highest grossing blockbusters of all time.

E.T. The Extra Terrestrial (1982)
US 41 × 27 in. (104 × 69 cm)
(Style A – Withdrawn)
Illustration by Drew Struzan
Photo by Steven Spielberg
Courtesy of the Martin Bridgewater Collection

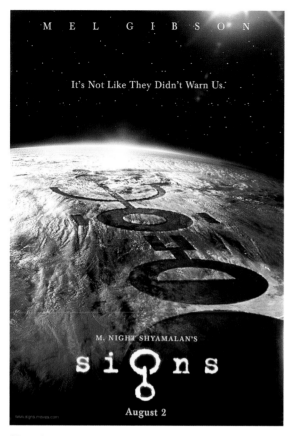

Signs (2002)
US 41 × 27 in. (104 × 69 cm)
(Advance)
Courtesy of the Andy Johnson Collection

The Arrival (1996)
US 41 × 27 in. (104 × 69 cm)
Art direction by Mark Crawford
Creative direction by Mark Crawford & Anthony Goldschmidt
Courtesy of the Andy Johnson Collection

The Arrival and *Signs* both play upon our age-old interest in the unknown and ask the question, 'Who or what is out there?' In both films, aliens are trying to infiltrate Earth by stealth and only a few humans seem to have noticed that the invasion of the planet is imminent.

When Steven Spielberg was a child his father used to wake him in the middle of a night to go and watch meteor showers. The director preserved his sense of wonder and excitement at space and the secrets it holds into adulthood, and this is vividly conveyed in his second blockbuster, *Close Encounters Of The Third Kind* (1977). (His first had been *Jaws* in 1975.)

Close Encounters Of The Third Kind was one of the top grossing films of 1977 and won a series of Academy Awards, not least for its special effects that combined cutting-edge technology with a clear vision. It is an uplifting film about peace and understanding, and the use of music to communicate with the aliens helps convey this beauty. Its optimistic idealism offered an escapist breath of fresh air in the economic malaise of the late seventies, and the film served to confirm that science fiction was a blockbuster genre.

A special 'UFO Facts' poster was released for the film. The information was actually provided by the Center for UFO Studies in Chicago, and indeed the poster invites interested readers to write to the Center for further information. The poster followed the success of a similar 'Shark Facts' poster for *Jaws* a few years previously.

We are not alone.

EVERY 15 MINUTES, SOMEONE SEES A UFO

UFOs — What are they?

The foremost authority on UFOs, Dr. J. Allen Hynek, astronomer, physicist, director of the Center for UFO Studies, defines a UFO: "The reported sighting of an object or light in the sky or on the land that *remains* unidentified after close study by technical experts, including authorities in aerospace, astronomy, and meteorology."

UFOs — A Global Phenomenon

Worldwide, there are an average of 100 sightings every 24 hours, one every fifteen minutes. About ten percent of these reports remain truly unidentified. From ancient and Biblical times, there have been extraordinary reports. In the last eighty years, the news media and then the scientific community have been noting these with expanding awareness. In 1897, UFOs were spotted in 20 states, witnessed by thousands in San Francisco, Kansas City, Omaha, Chicago, St. Louis. In World War Two, Allied, German and Japanese bomber pilots described "blobs of light" and "disc-shaped objects" travelling at incredible speeds. In 1947, the term "flying saucer" became part of the language. Sightings continue to be reported from every region of the world.

UFOs — All Shapes and Sizes

In addition to the "flying saucer," descriptions have included "luminous tear drops," "diamond-shaped objects," elongated rectangles," "daylight discs," "nocturnal lights." Sizes vary from only a few feet in diameter to "ships as big as a football field."

UFOs — Peak Months, Peak Hours

The largest number of reported sightings are between 9:00 p.m. and 3:00 a.m. with the peak months July, August, and October, even in those parts of the world whose seasons are the reverse of ours.

UFOs — Seen by 15 Million Americans

They include leaders in science, the space program, astronomy, and government, as well as military and airline pilots, doctors, teachers, law enforcement officers, and ordinary people from every walk of life in every part of the country.

UFOs — Close Encounters. What Are They?

Dr. Hynek has categorized these encounters into three classifications:

Close Encounters of the First Kind:

Sighting of a UFO at very close range but no interaction with the environment other than trauma on the part of the observer.

Close Encounters of the Second Kind:

Physical evidence found at the site of a UFO. These include effects on animals and inanimate material; burn marks; vegetation pressed down; car engines killed; lights lowered or extinguished. In such cases, vehicles reportedly return to normal operation after the UFO is gone.

Close Encounters of the Third Kind:

Contact with the occupants of a UFO. This is the most extraordinary of the Close Encounters, actual sighting and contact with "UFO beings."

CLOSE ENCOUNTERS
OF THE THIRD KIND

For further information on UFOs
send a stamped self-addressed envelope to The
Center For UFO Studies, 924 Chicago Avenue, Evanston, IL 60202

THIS SPECIAL REPORT PROVIDED AS A PUBLIC SERVICE BY THE PRODUCERS OF "CLOSE ENCOUNTERS OF THE THIRD KIND."

PRINTED IN U.S.A.

1 SHEET

Close Encounters Of The Third Kind (1977)
US 41 × 27 in. (104 × 69 cm)
(UFO Facts)
Courtesy of the James Moores Collection

Botschaft Der Gotter
(In Search Of Ancient Astronauts / Poskannictwo Z Innej Planety) (1973)
Polish 23 × 33 in. (58 × 84 cm)
Art by Jerzy Flisak
Courtesy of The Reel Poster Gallery

It is a common misconception that UFOs are a twentieth-century phenomenon. In fact, as early as the fifteenth century BC, Egyptian Thutmose III was claiming to have seen 'foul smelling circles of fire and discs in the sky' and there are several well-attested cases of ancient tribes from Africa to Australia who seem to have acquired an inexplicably detailed knowledge of astronomy long before the first telescope was invented. Many people claim to believe that visitors from distant planets have played key roles in humanity's development and *Botschaft Der Gotter* sets out to investigate this theory.

During the 1940s, sightings of UFOs reached new and alarming levels. Significant numbers of World War II pilots reported seeing luminescent cylinders or spheres in the sky (the term 'Foo Fighter' was coined to describe the phenomenon). In America, the authorities were receiving so many reports of UFO sightings that Project Sign was established by the government in January 1948 to investigate these strange happenings. *Unidentified Flying Objects* is a docu-drama that discusses this intriguing period in the history of flying saucers.

● **1947**. Kenneth Arnold makes the first nationally reported UFO sighting. Two weeks later the US military disclose then retract the famous 'disc' story at Roswell.

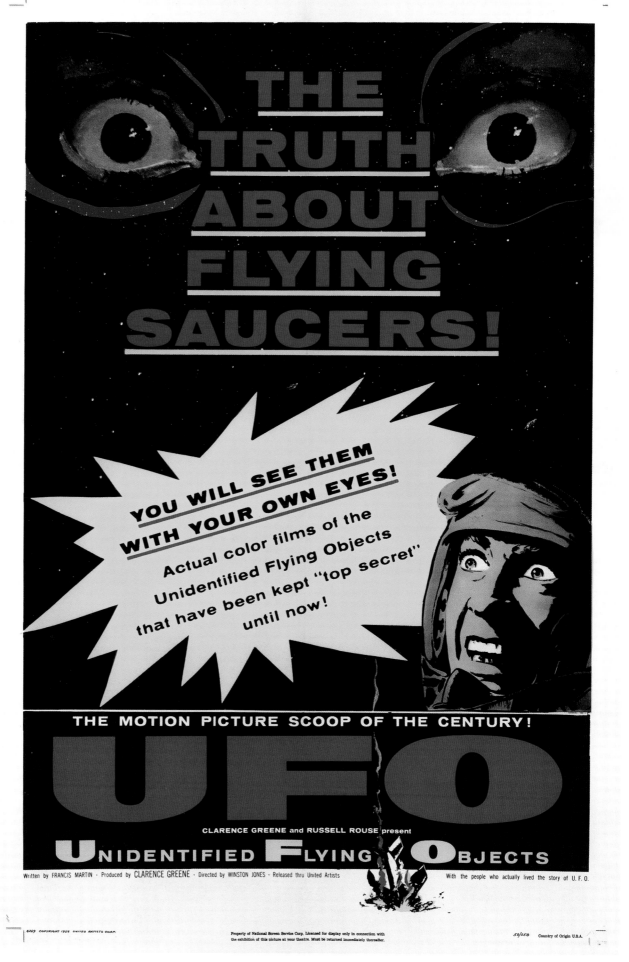

Unidentified Flying Objects: The True Story Of Flying Saucers / UFO (1956)
US 41 × 27 in. (104 × 69 cm)
Courtesy of the Andy Johnson Collection

The FANTASTIC Night Of TERROR That Menaced The Fate Of The World!

"DEVIL GIRL FROM MARS"

starring
Hugh McDermott · Hazel Court · Peter Reynolds · Adrienne Corri
Joseph Tomelty · Sophie Stewart · John Laurie · Patricia Laffan
Directed by David MacDonald · Produced by Edward J. Danziger and
Harry Lee Danziger · A Spartan Release

Devil Girl From Mars (1954)
US 81 × 41 in. (206 × 104 cm)
Courtesy of The Haldane Collection

The Man From Planet X is set on a desolate Scottish island where a benevolent alien lands, looking for help for his dying planet. Far from offering assistance, however, the people who receive him are interested only in exploiting him for their own ends. In *Devil Girl From Mars*, on the other hand, it is the alien dominatrix, Nyah, and her robot who are the baddies. They have come to Scotland (again!) looking for men to take back to Mars for breeding purposes. The film, which had its tongue firmly in its cheek, was a British satire on *The Day The Earth Stood Still* (1951).

The Man From Planet X (1951)
US 41 × 27 in. (104 × 69 cm)
Courtesy of the Andy Johnson Collection

The Thing From Another World (1951)
US 41 × 27 in. (104 × 69 cm)

The Thing From Another World (1951)
US 36 × 14 in. (91 × 36 cm)

The Thing From Another World is a successful fusion of science fiction and horror. Based on the 1948 story *Who Goes There?* by science fiction writer John E. Campbell Jr, it is an intelligent film set in the desolate arctic where a group of research scientists discover an alien frozen in the ice for thousands of years. After they have accidentally defrosted it, the alien embarks upon a killing spree in the base. Although the monster appears in the form of a man, it is in fact a carnivorous vegetable. In contrast, in John Carpenter's remake and re-adaptation of Campbell's story in 1982, simply titled *The Thing*, the alien is a shape-shifter which assumes the likeness of its victim. This gives the film a chilling and paranoid dimension.

The standard American poster, and the larger American posters for the original version of *The Thing*, are simple in design, suggesting the horrific nature of the film by the use of blood-coloured lettering and veins spiralling across the paper. The smaller posters for the film use similar lettering but with the addition of scenes from the movie. The blood-like mass in the background of the British eighties poster is suggestive of the fate suffered by the monster's victims, while the small figures marching slowly across the snow symbolize the lonely and desolate setting of the film.

The Thing (1982)
British 41 × 27 in. (104 × 69 cm)
Courtesy of The Reel Poster Gallery

Invaders From Mars (Gli Invasori Spaziali) (1953)
Italian 55 × 39 in. (140 × 99 cm)

Invaders From Mars epitomizes the red scare movie of the fifties. Martians land in a little boy's sandpit and quickly start replacing the adults around him with unfeeling replicas. He enlists the help of the attractive Dr Blake and together they confront the invaders in the inevitable 'good triumphs over evil' finale. Like the film, the American poster, and the smaller Italian one, are very traditional and represent classic B-movie poster art. In contrast, Renato Fratini's larger design is an abstract and unique artwork that is avant-garde even by modern standards. It stands as one of the most artistic and interesting science fiction designs in film poster art.

Invaders From Mars (1953)
US 41 × 27 in. (104 × 69 cm)

Invaders From Mars (Gli Invasori Spaziali) (1953)
Italian 79 × 55 in. (201 × 140 cm)
Art by Renato Fratini
Courtesy of The Haldane Collection

Invasion Of The Body Snatchers (1956)
US 22 × 28 in. (56 × 71 cm)
(Style B)
Courtesy of the Steve Smith Collection

Shot in nineteen days on a low budget, *Invasion Of The Body Snatchers* projects a sophistication and subtlety missing in more 'gung-ho gore' science fiction films of the decade. Using Jack Finney's 1954 novel as its basis, *Invasion Of The Body Snatchers* can be seen not only as a metaphor for the threat of communism, but also as a commentary on the bland conformity of American suburbia during the time of McCarthyism. The tension is steadily racked up as the citizens of a small Californian town are replaced, one by one, by their doppelgangers. These alien life-forms grow from plant-like pods to assume the likeness of anyone they choose. That person is then replaced by a psychically identical, but emotionless, replica. The growing paranoia and sense of menace are palpable as the central protagonists seek to escape an unseen and omnipresent enemy.

The pods are clearly intended to highlight the dangers of allowing one's feelings and emotion to be suppressed. Don Siegel, the film's director, states that 'To be a pod means that you have no passion, no anger, that you talk automatically, that the spark of life has left you.' Ultimately, the film is, perhaps, a challenge to embrace life while we have the chance.

Influencing a host of science fiction films to the present day, *Invasion Of The Body Snatchers* was remade in 1978 and again in 1993 as *Body Snatchers*.

Invasion Of The Body Snatchers (1956)
US 36 × 14 in. (91 × 36 cm)
Courtesy of The Reel Poster Gallery

20 Million Miles To Earth (A 30 Milioni Di Km. Dalla Terra) (1957)
Italian 55 × 39 in. (140 × 99 cm)
Art by Anselmo Ballester
Courtesy of The Reel Poster Gallery

Ray Harryhausen (b. 1920) stands alongside Willis O'Brien as one of the greatest stop-motion animators in cinema and he has had a massive impact on the development of special effects in the twentieth century. After seeing *King Kong* (1933) at the age of thirteen, the young Harryhausen developed a passion for stop-motion techniques, even contacting O'Brien to ask his advice on a short film that he had made. Such determination paid off and his first job came a few years later, working with George Pal on his Puppetoon shorts for Paramount. After the war, he landed a job with his hero, O'Brien, on *Mighty Joe Young* (1949). The majority of animation was, in fact, Harryhausen's work, with O'Brien focusing more on production. In the early fifties, Harryhausen developed a stop-motion technique that lowered the cost of special effects and allowed them to be incorporated into relatively low budget productions, the first of which was *The Beast From 20,000 Fathoms* (1953). He then teamed up with producer Charles Schneer to produce a series of films that are remembered even today as landmarks in the history of special effects; they include *It Came From Beneath The Sea* (1955), *Earth Vs. The Flying Saucers* (1956) and *20 Million Miles To Earth* (1957). Ray Harryhausen was awarded an honorary Oscar for his contribution to the development of special effects in 1992.

20 Million Miles To Earth is remembered for its fantastic special effects by Ray Harryhausen, and his monster is the real star of the film. Unfortunately, the creature was sidelined on the American domestic poster campaign. In contrast, Anselmo Ballester's artwork offers a wonderful portrayal of the beast. The film itself begins when an American spaceship crash-lands in the sea off a small Sicilian fishing village, astonishing the inhabitants. Again, Ballester's depiction of the scene is striking and conveys the dramatic impact of the falling rocket. Inside the spacecraft, a small boy discovers a mass of goo which, after he takes it to a friendly zoologist, turns into a monster and begins to grow at an alarming rate. The creature, which Harryhausen named the Ymir after the father of all giants from Norse mythology, is soon twenty feet long and on the loose in the streets of Rome. Essentially innocent, the monster is eventually killed by electrocution.

20 Million Miles To Earth (A 30 Milioni Di Km. Dalla Terra) (1957)
Italian 79 × 55 in. (201 × 140 cm)
Art by Anselmo Ballester
Courtesy of The Reel Poster Gallery

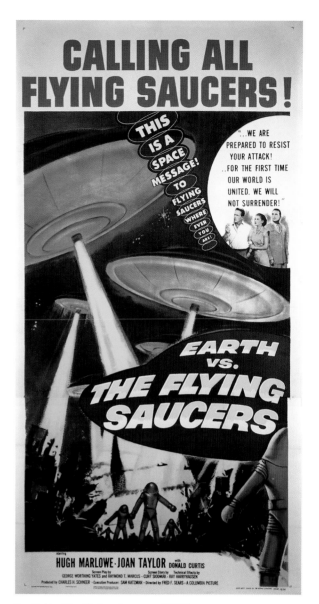

Earth Vs. The Flying Saucers
(La Terra Contro I Dischi Volanti) (1956)
Italian 79 × 55 in. (201 × 140 cm)
Art by Anselmo Ballester
Courtesy of the Peter & Betty Langs Collection

Earth Vs. The Flying Saucers (1956)
US 81 × 41 in. (206 × 104 cm)

Earth Vs. The Flying Saucers has the ideal combination of B-movie naivety and fantastic special effects to give it lasting appeal. The fifties was a golden age in American history where anything seemed possible, including the appearance of alien beings on city streets. The news report and documentary-style voice-over with which the film opens plays on this idea, and the American poster took up the same theme, designed to read like a news report. The plot is traditional – aliens land on earth bent on destruction and humanity faces a fight for survival in a decisive battle of good against evil – and, like most fifties science fiction, it has distinct cold war undertones. To audiences living at a time when American-Soviet relations were dominated by the doctrines of massive retaliation and mutually assured destruction, it came as no surprise when Earth fired the first shot at the aliens, assuming them to be hostile – it was a cardinal cold war principle that, wherever possible, it was prudent to get your retaliation in first! But what distinguishes *Earth Vs. The Flying Saucers* from its many contemporaries are the special effects, which add a convincing reality to the story. Ray Harryhausen created a fleet of flying saucers that are seen hovering over every city in the world and the UFOs are shown on every campaign poster for the film. Anselmo Ballester's designs are typical; one, traditionally realistic in style, shows the saucers destroying London's Big Ben, while his other design, again showing the saucers, is more abstract and colourful. The final battle between Earth and the flying saucers, set in Washington, DC, is brilliant and obviously inspired similar scenes in the nineties blockbuster, *Independence Day* (1996).

Earth Vs. The Flying Saucers (La Terra Contro I Dischi Volanti) (1956)
Italian 55 × 39 in. (140 × 99 cm)
Art by Anselmo Ballester
Courtesy of The Reel Poster Gallery

Independence Day (1996)
US 41 × 27 in. (104 × 69 cm)
(Style B)
Courtesy of The Reel Poster Gallery

Independence Day (1996)
US 41 × 27 in. (104 × 69 cm)
(Advance Style B)
Courtesy of The Reel Poster Gallery

Independence Day is essentially a fifties science fiction film with a contemporary twist and the realistic 'photography' used on the posters effectively illustrates how far digital technology has allowed effects to advance since the 1950s. The plot owes much to both *The War Of The Worlds* (1953) and *Earth Vs. The Flying Saucers* (1956), and has Will Smith, Jeff Goldblum and the supporting cast struggling against enormous and apparently invincible alien spaceships in yet another struggle to save the world from annihilation.

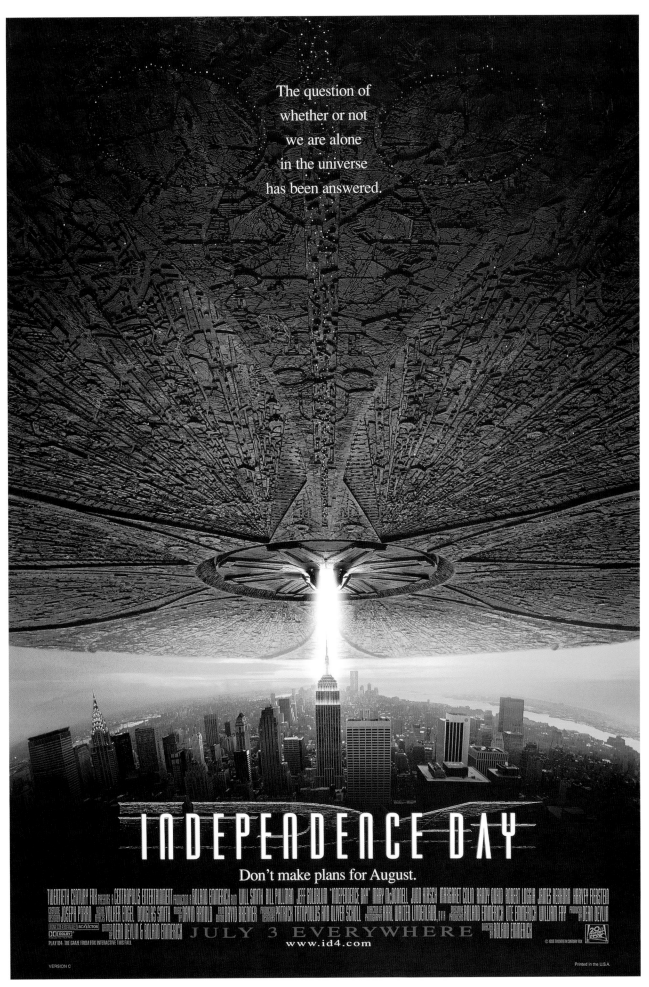

Independence Day (1996)
US 41 × 27 in. (104 × 69 cm)
(Style C)
Courtesy of the Andy Johnson Collection

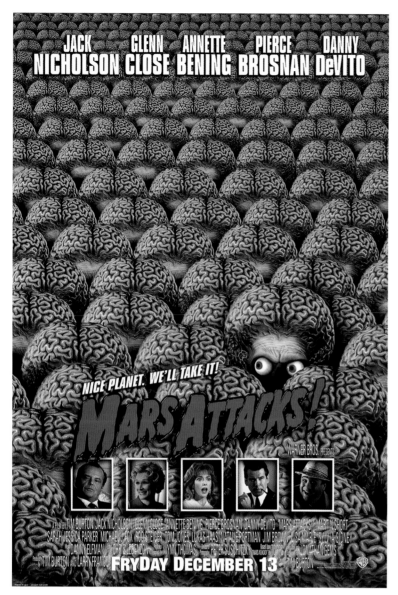

Mars Attacks! (1996)
US 41 × 27 in. (104 × 69 cm)
(Advance)
Art direction and design by Charles Reimers
Courtesy of The Reel Poster Gallery

Mars Attacks! (1996)
US 41 × 27 in. (104 × 69 cm)
(International)
Art by Philip Castle
Courtesy of The Reel Poster Gallery

Mars Attacks! pays homage to the science fiction films of the fifties and sixties and this is reflected in the poster designs. With an amazingly impressive cast, the film has a perverse humour that has already attracted a cult following. The film is based on a series of bubble gum collectible cards issued by the Topps Company in 1962. (To preserve the firm's reputation and because of the contentious nature of the material, the cards were in fact issued under the name 'Bubbles, Inc.') The cards were gruesome and bloody and the company faced such a barrage of parental complaints and so much bad press that production was cut short and the cards instantly became collectibles.

Mars Attacks! (1996)
US 41 × 27 in. (104 × 69 cm)
(International Style B)
Design by Andrew Percival & Charles Reimers
Courtesy of The Reel Poster Gallery

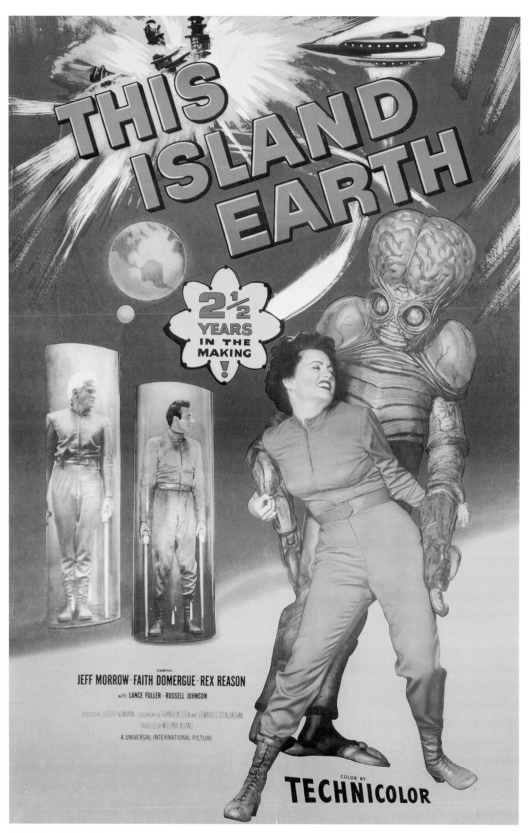

This Island, Earth (1955)
US 60 × 40 in. (152 × 102 cm)
(Style B)

Fifties science fiction is populated by monsters and aliens. These fantastic creatures, state-of-the-art in their time, now appear strangely dated, especially on the screen where the limited special effects often produced monsters that were more risible than terrifying. But the poster artists, free from technological limitations, were able to preserve the full splendour of the scriptwriters' weird and wonderful imaginations. *This Island, Earth* and *Invasion Of The Saucer Men* are two of the best examples of the genre.

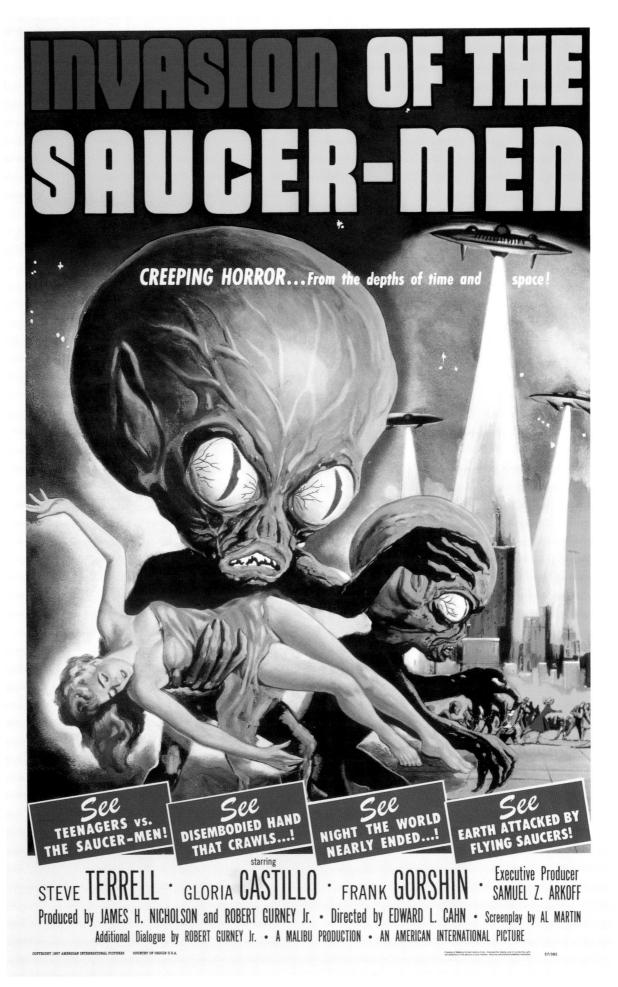

Invasion Of The Saucer Men (1957)
US 41 × 27 in. (104 × 69 cm)
Art by Albert Kallis
Courtesy of The Reel Poster Gallery

Forbidden Planet is one of an elite group of fifties science fiction films that can truly claim cult status. With a story-line based loosely on Shakespeare's *The Tempest*, the film is most famous for its fantastic special effects and for Robby the Robot, a friendly machine that protects the planet. The film had a huge influence on Gene Roddenberry's *Star Trek* and on Lucas's androids in *Star Wars*. The image of Robby carrying a woman is an icon and was adapted for posters around the world. Ironically, Averardo Ciriello's design for the Italian poster has Robby carrying a man. This is unusual for the Italian artists, who are renowned for inserting nubile, swooning females whenever possible.

Forbidden Planet (Il Pianeta Proibito) (1956)
Italian 55 × 39 in. (140 × 99 cm)
Art by Averardo Ciriello

Forbidden Planet (1956)
US 41 × 27 in. (104 × 69 cm)
Courtesy of The Reel Poster Gallery

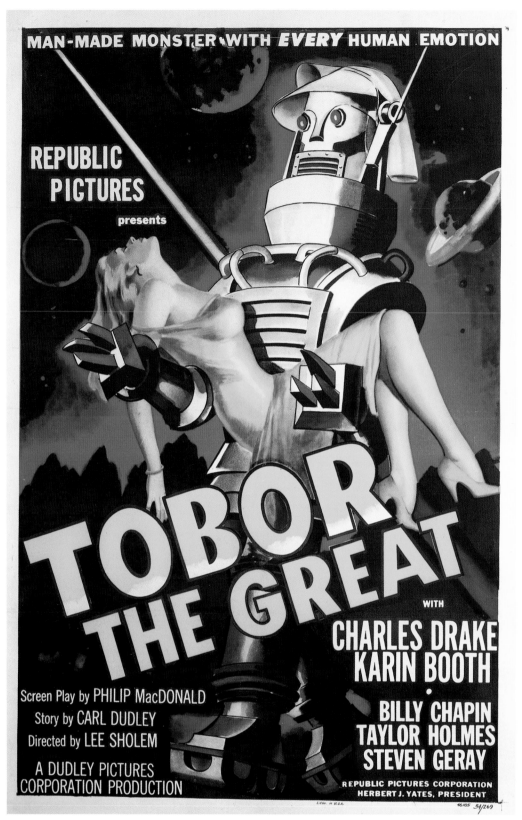

Tobor The Great (1954)
US 41 × 27 in. (104 × 69 cm)

The classic concept of a robot, a lumbering, mechanical caricature of a human being, existed until the invention of the more human android in the seventies, and such robots were a staple of science fiction films. *Der Herr Der Welt* is one of the earlier examples and, for a film made in Adolf Hitler's Germany, has a message that is surprisingly anti-technology. The plot concerns a scientist's assistant who develops a robot that starts killing those closest to it; the robots then proliferate and threaten to take over the world. Two decades later the classical robot was in its heyday, playing a starring role in numerous science fiction films such as *Tobor The Great*; the extent of this movie's sophistication is reflected by the fact that the title is simply robot spelt backwards.

Der Herr Der Welt (Master Of The World) (1934)
German 56 × 38 in. (142 × 97 cm)
Art by A. M. Cay

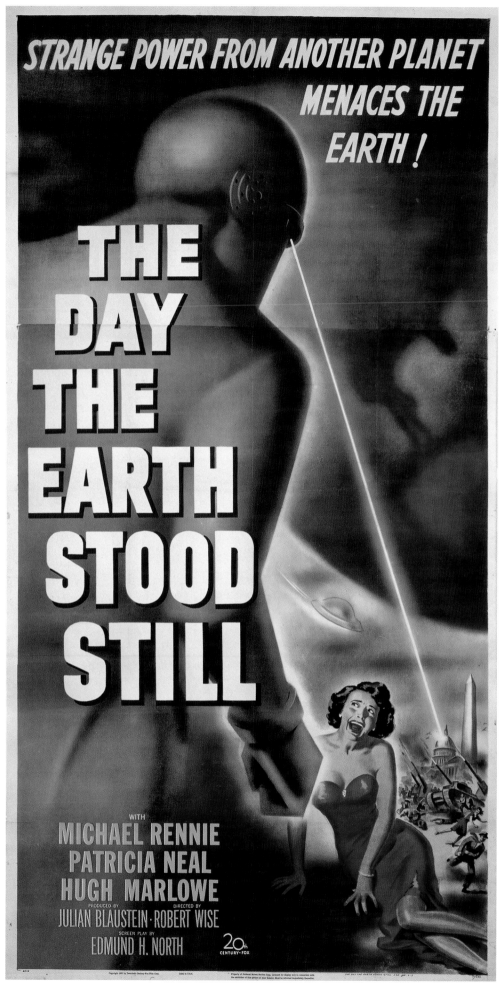

The Day The Earth Stood Still (1951)
US 81 × 41 in. (206 × 104 cm)
Courtesy of the Andrew Cohen Collection

The Day The Earth Stood Still is a poignant film about disarmament, and a daring one, given that it was released in the frosty depths of the cold war. Based on the novella *Farewell To Arms* (1940) by Harry Bates, it tells the story of Klaatu, an alien who lands on Earth with his robot Gort. Klaatu brings a message of peace for all humanity and demands that all atomic weapons be destroyed. After the leaders of the world reject his appeal, Klaatu demonstrates his authority by cutting off all non-essential power across the world, forcing everyone to stand still long enough to hear his ultimatum: if the nations refuse to heed him, then Gort will be forced to destroy the planet. The film's anti-nuclear message is blunt, and it is unusual for the period in that the aliens are portrayed as intelligent and peace-loving as opposed to a barbaric, war-mongering humanity. The serious message and content of the film was atypical of fifties science fiction. However, this was ignored on the poster designs which show the standard innocent damsel in distress being terrorized by an alien of unequivocally evil aspect.

The Day The Earth Stood Still (1951)
US 41 × 27 in. (104 × 69 cm)
Courtesy of The Reel Poster Gallery

Robocop (Robotzsaru) (1987)
Hungarian 33 × 23 in. (84 × 58 cm)
Art by Heleny
Courtesy of The Reel Poster Gallery

While the Western world has apparently become obsessed with perfecting the human physique, science has, at the same time, made it possible to build elaborate prostheses and other artificial body parts to replace or enhance bits of the human anatomy. *Robocop* projects these two trends into the future to a time when it has become possible to construct the ultimate being – an android that combines robotic strength with human guile. This idea is vividly captured in the Hungarian poster for the film and, indeed, what makes Robocop a hero is not his strength but his humanity. In contrast, *The Terminator* is an emotionless automaton and this is reflected in the Czechoslovakian poster. Arnold Schwarzenegger, described in the *Guinness Book of Records* as 'the most perfectly developed man in the history of the world', was the perfect choice to play the robot. The film established him as one of the greatest action heroes of the eighties and proved such a success that director James Cameron brought him back in a friendlier guise in *Terminator II: Judgment Day* (1991).

- **1931.** American Society of Plastic and Reconstructive Surgeons is formed.
- **1962.** Thomas Cronin introduces the use of silicon to make breast implants.
- **1997.** 'Deep Blue', the IBM computer, beats Garry Kasparov at chess.

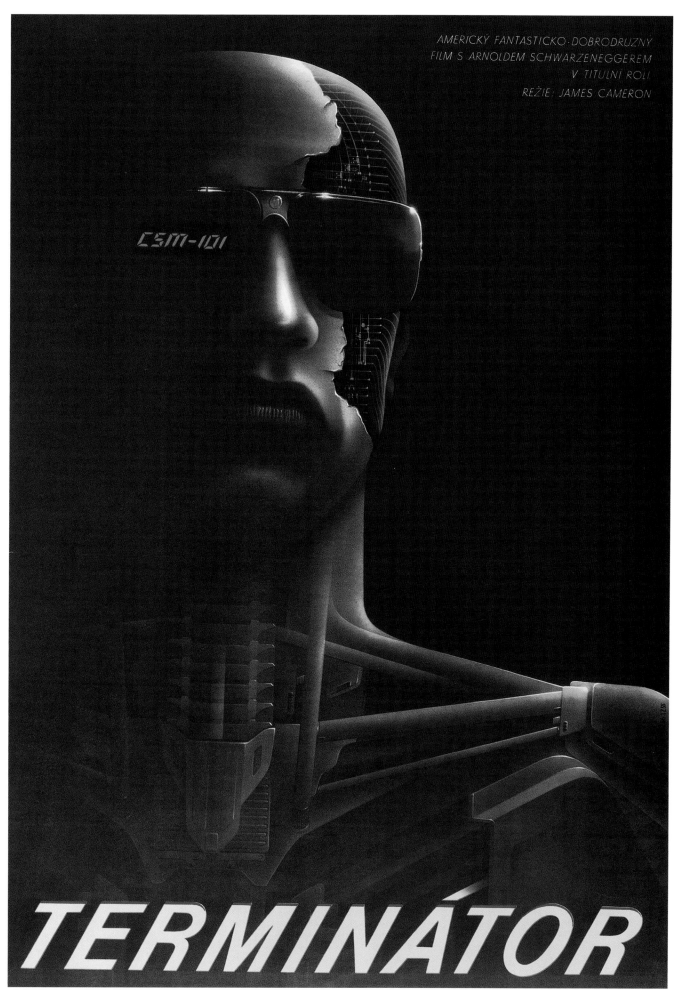

AMERICKÝ FANTASTICKO-DOBRODRUZNÝ
FILM S ARNOLDEM SCHWARZENEGGEREM
V TITULNÍ ROLI.
REŽIE: JAMES CAMERON

CSM-101

TERMINÁTOR

The Terminator (Terminátor) (1984)
Czechoslovakian 33 × 23 in. (84 × 58 cm)
Courtesy of The Reel Poster Gallery

Westworld (Swiat Dzikiego Zachodu) (1973)
Polish 33 × 23 in. (84 × 58 cm)
Art by Jan Mlodozeniec
Courtesy of the Mark Faulkner Collection

Westworld is a bleak and menacing blend of science fiction and western. The film is set in the near future in a remote and exclusive island theme park; a world where fantasies come true and nothing can go wrong! Two businessmen head to the Wild West section of the park to shoot it out with cowboys and woo the local gals. It is simple amusement until a rogue robot malfunctions and starts a killing spree on the island. The film climaxes in a dramatic showdown between the hero and the automaton.

Westworld was written and directed by **Michael Crichton** (b. 1942). Famous for his best-selling 'techno-thriller' novels, he is also responsible for the hit television series *ER*. (His years spent at Harvard studying medicine provided ample material.) He has converted a number of his works into movies; *The Andromeda Strain* (1971), *Coma* (1978) and *Jurassic Park* (1993) are three examples in the science fiction genre.

Westworld (1973)
US 41 × 27 in. (104 × 69 cm)
(International)
Courtesy of The Reel Poster Gallery

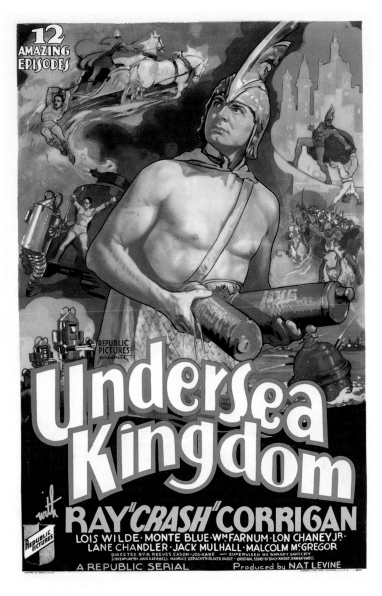

Undersea Kingdom (1936)
US 41 × 27 in. (104 × 69 cm)

The Phantom Empire (1935)
US 81 × 41 in. (206 × 104 cm)

Between 1929 and 1956, over 200 serials were made in Hollywood, mostly by Universal, Republic and Columbia. Their casts included many actors who would in due course become stars, and occasionally they created a new star, as was the case with Larry 'Buster' Crabbe in the role of *Flash Gordon*. The serials were often adapted from popular radio programmes or comic strips, and were made up of anything between twelve and fifteen chapters. They played before the main feature in theatres and the cliff-hanger chapter-endings brought audiences back week after week.

Originally playing over twelve successive Saturday afternoons, *The Phantom Empire* (1935) is one of the more bizarre examples of a chapter serial. The plot is a surreal mix of western and science fiction in which Gene Autry stars as a singing cowboy who discovers a technologically advanced underground world beneath his radium-rich ranch and successfully helps the peaceful inhabitants to fight off the greedy, unscrupulous villains on the surface.

Undersea Kingdom (1936) starred stuntman and action hero Ray 'Crash' Corrigan, complete with crash helmet. Corrigan, with beautiful girl and clever professor in tow, goes beneath the waves to investigate the source of a series of earthquakes. There the team discovers the lost city of Atlantis, whose inhabitants, the noble, white-caped Atlanteans, are embroiled in a bitter war against their evil, black-caped adversaries. Just as in *The Phantom Empire*, the visitors from the surface must rid the subterranean realm of evil and restore peace once again.

The Master Mystery (1919)
US 41 × 27 in. (104 × 69 cm)
(Chapter 13)

Flash Gordon (1936)
US 81 × 41 in. (206 × 104 cm)
Courtesy of The Reel Poster Gallery

Created by Alex Raymond and Don Moore as a rival to the *Buck Rogers* comic strip, *Flash Gordon* made its first appearance on paper in January 1934 and was adapted for the screen two years later. Crabbe played the role in three serials between 1936 and 1940: *Flash Gordon* (1936), *Flash Gordon's Trip To Mars* (1938) and *Flash Gordon Conquers the Universe* (1940). All feature Flash and his girlfriend Dale Arden frustrating the evil designs of Ming The Merciless.

Flash Gordon (1936)
US 81 × 81 in. (206 × 206 cm)
Courtesy of The Reel Poster Gallery

Flash Gordon's Trip To Mars (1938)
US 41 × 27 in. (104 × 69 cm)
(Chapter 12: Ming The Merciless)

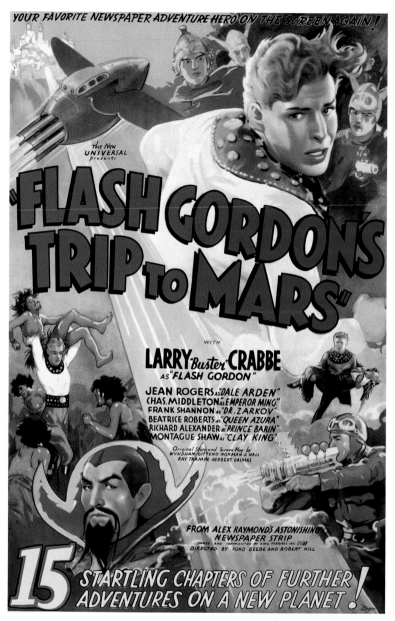

Flash Gordon's Trip To Mars (1938)
US 41 × 27 in. (104 × 69 cm)

Although each serial averaged twelve chapters, the studios would print one poster to launch the series and this would be printed in full colour. They would produce a new poster, usually in two colours, for each chapter, carrying both the serial title and the title of the individual chapter. *Ming The Merciless* is an example of a chapter poster.

Flash Gordon Conquers The Universe (1940)
US 41 × 27 in. (104 × 69 cm)
Courtesy of The Reel Poster Gallery

Rocket Ship (1938)
US 81 × 41 in. (206 × 104 cm)
Courtesy of The Reel Poster Gallery

Rocket Ship is a feature-length film that was created by combining material from the first two *Flash Gordon* serials. Flash and Dale must travel in their rocket ship to the planet Mongo in order to confront Ming The Merciless and prevent him from destroying Earth.

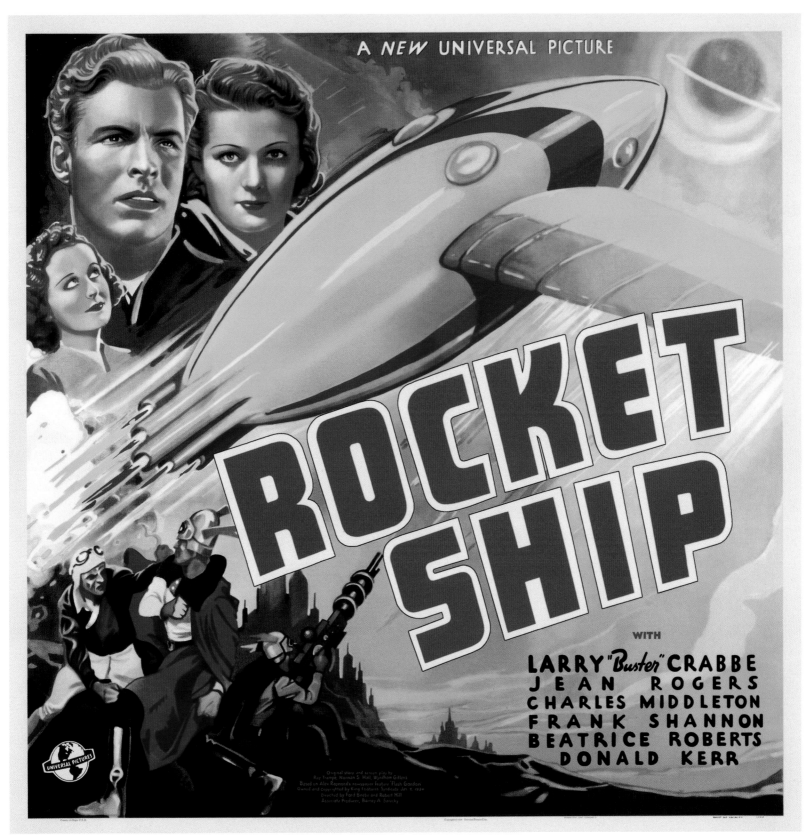

Rocket Ship (1938)
US 81 × 81 in. (206 × 206 cm)
Courtesy of The Reel Poster Gallery

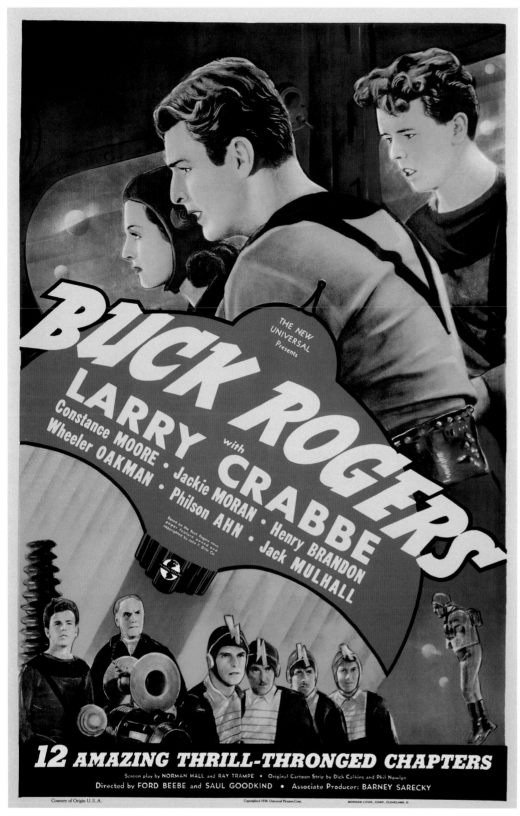

Buck Rogers (1939)
US 41 × 27 in. (104 × 69 cm)

Buck Rogers first appeared as Anthony Rogers in *Armageddon – 2419 A.D.* by Philip Francis Nowlan, published in the August 1928 issue of *Amazing Stories*. Nowlan was subsequently commissioned, with the help of artist Richard Calkins, to turn Anthony Rogers into the world's first science fiction comic strip hero. When the Buck Rogers strip began appearing in the national press it was an instant hit. The transition to the screen proved equally successful. Buster Crabbe, the star of *Flash Gordon*, played the title role and the films are so similar that it is often assumed they are parts of a single series.

Captain Marvel first appeared in *Whiz Comics* in 1940. Republic's serial of his adventures in 1941 is widely regarded as one of the best in the field, with remarkable stunts and wonderful special effects. A dying wizard imparts his power to Billy, a young boy who then only has to shout 'Shazam!' in order to be transformed into Captain Marvel, 'the world's mightiest mortal'. The typical serial chapter endings – 'Will our hero make it on time?', 'Is this the end of our hero?' – all recur at regular intervals throughout this twelve-chapter tale of scorpions, Egyptian curses and other exotic perils.

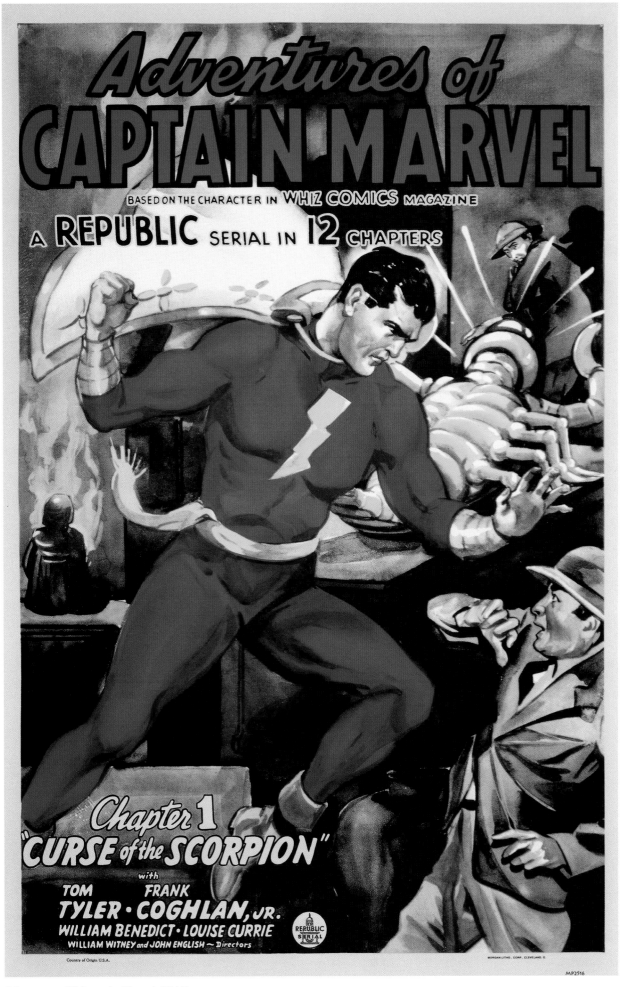

Adventures Of Captain Marvel (1941)
US 41 × 27 in. (104 × 69 cm)
(Chapter 1: Curse of the Scorpion)

Batman And Robin (1964)
US 41 × 27 in. (104 × 69 cm)

Batman first appeared in *Detective Comics* in May 1939. A self-made superhero, Batman battles evil and protects the innocent using his characteristic combination of physical prowess and mysterious powers. His boy-wonder sidekick Robin joined his adventures in April 1940. The duo first appeared on the screen in a 1943 serial, reappeared in a fifteen-chapter serial in 1949 and were again serialized in the sixties. Batman has proved one of the most enduring action heroes and has starred in a whole series of feature-length films from the sixties to the present day.

Batman And Robin (1949)
US 81 × 81 in. (206 × 206 cm)

Superman (1948)
US 41 × 27 in. (104 × 69 cm)

Superman (1941–43)
US 41 × 27 in. (104 × 69 cm)
(Stock poster)

Superman, the prototypical superhero, was created by Jerry Siegel and Joe Schuster and made his first appearance in *Action Comics* in June 1938. Although many other superheroes would later follow in his footsteps, or fly in his wake, Superman's financial success remains unchallenged. Before his live screen debut in 1948, Superman starred in a series of cartoons in the early forties with animation by Max Fleischer. The generic posters for these cartoons had a space at the bottom in which the cinema operator could fill in the title and other information relating to the particular cartoon that was to be presented. This enabled the same design to be reused week after week.

Max Fleischer (1883–1973) was for years Walt Disney's only serious rival. He started as a newspaper cartoonist before progressing to screen animation. Fleischer pioneered a number of techniques, most notably using real, live-action footage as a basis for making moving cartoons. His brother Dave was used as the basis for Koko the Clown and, together, the brothers turned Koko into a series of *Out Of The Inkwell* cartoons. In the mid-twenties Max started working on the first 'talking' cartoons and invented the 'bouncing ball' – a device that allowed viewers to sing along to lyrics projected on to the screen. The famously flirty and risqué *Betty Boop* was another success for Fleischer, as was his studio's adaptation of Elzie Segar's *Popeye*. In the early forties he took on the challenge of adapting the established comic-book strip *Superman* into a series of cartoons for the big screen.

Superman (1948)
US 81 × 41 in. (206 × 104 cm)
Courtesy of the Tarek AbuZayyad Collection

Superman: The Movie (1978)
US 36 × 14 in. (91 × 36 cm)
Art by Bob Peak
Courtesy of The Reel Poster Gallery

Superheroes are an integral part of American popular culture. They have a timeless appeal that works equally well on paper as on the big screen, and they remain as popular today as in the past. Starring Christopher Reeve as the man of steel, *Superman: The Movie* (1978) introduced the original superhero to a new generation of film-goers, and its success gave rise to three sequels in the eighties. The character was so well established in the popular imagination that Bob Peak's simple use of the shield logo on the poster was all that was needed to market the movie. (For Bob Peak, see p. 30.)

Superman was nearing his twenty-fifth birthday when Spider-Man made his debut in *Marvel Comics* in 1963. The brainchild of Stan Lee, Spider-Man's charm stems from the contrast between teenage awkwardness and superhero cool. A blockbuster adaptation of *Spider-Man* was released in 2002 and this is the first poster from the campaign. The second advance is identical in design, but only has '2002' printed across the bottom. Both posters are double-sided and have a high gloss finish. Both were pulled from circulation in August 2001 because of the unauthorized use of the image of New York's Chrysler building. With the dispute resolved, a third advance poster was released with the same image and the words, '3 May 2002'. It was this third print that was withdrawn after September 11, 2001 because the appearance of the Twin Towers' reflection in Spider-Man's goggles was deemed inappropriate.

Spider-Man (2002)
US 41 × 27 in. (104 × 69 cm)
(Advance Style A – Withdrawn)
Courtesy of the Andy Johnson Collection

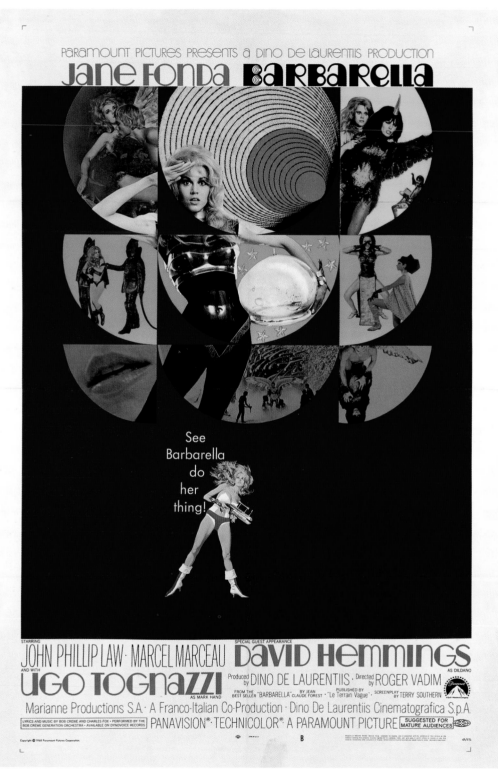

Barbarella is a cult classic and the variety of colourful and entertaining poster designs from around the world reflect this status. The Japanese and alternate US poster are both in the spirit of the psychedelic sixties and reflects the sexual revolution which was another feature of the decade.

Barbarella (1968)
US 41 × 27 in. (104 × 69 cm)
(Style B)
Courtesy of The Reel Poster Gallery

Barbarella (1968)
Japanese 30 × 20 in. (76 × 51 cm)

Star Wars (1977)
US 41 × 27 in. (104 × 69 cm)
(Style D)
Art by Drew Struzan & Charles White III
Courtesy of The Reel Poster Gallery

Star Wars was the film that changed the face of science-fiction cinema by establishing its enormous commercial potential and permanently raising the genre to family blockbuster status.

George Lucas conceived and wrote the story in 1975. He divided the tale into two trilogies and then approached Hollywood with the first. Twentieth Century Fox was the only studio willing to take on the project, which was viewed as a ludicrously naïve venture unlikely to make money. By the end of its first theatrical run, *Star Wars* was the highest grossing film in American history. (*The Empire Strikes Back* and *Return Of The Jedi* proved equally profitable.) Lucas then made a nebulous promise to make a Prequel Trilogy some time in the future. Fifteen years later, *Phantom Menace* was released, again breaking all previous records with the largest single day's gross in history.

From a variety of countries of origin, *Star Wars* poster art encompasses numerous styles and approaches to poster design by many talented artists.

Star Wars (1977)
US 41 × 27 in. (104 × 69 cm)
(Style A)
Art by Tom Jung
Courtesy of the Andy Johnson Collection

Star Wars (1977)
British 30 × 40 in. (76 × 102 cm)
(First version – Withdrawn)
Art by Tim and Greg Hildebrandt
Courtesy of The Reel Poster Gallery

Rarely has a collaborative design team proved more fruitful and productive than that of **Tim and Greg Hildebrandt** (b. 1939). The identical twins were born in Detroit, Michigan and studied at Meinzingers School of Art. With a legendary reputation in the field of fantasy art, the brothers work in acrylics on hardboard. Their technique involves each twin starting at one end of the painting, meeting in the middle and then returning to work on detail. However unorthodox, this remarkable approach is obviously successful!

The brothers' artwork for *Star Wars* was commissioned before the phenomenon took off on a global scale. Although the image they created was used for merchandising in the States, it was originally intended principally for use on the British poster. However, in the six months that elapsed between the film's release in America and its arrival in Britain, the studio bosses became dissatisfied with an artwork that bore no resemblance to the actors involved. Very few of the original Hildebrandt design were printed. Instead, Twentieth Century Fox hired the British illustrator, **Tom William Chantrell** (1916–2001) to design a poster with characters that were clearly recognizable as Mark Hamill, Harrison Ford and Carrie Fisher. It was this design that was used for the final British quad and Chantrell's poster was also adapted for the Style C (International) American poster.

Star Wars (1977)
US 41 × 27 in. (104 × 69 cm)
(Style C – International)
Art by Tom William Chantrell
Courtesy of the Andy Johnson Collection

George Lucas had a clear and determined vision for marketing *Star Wars* and this included a merchandising campaign for the film. One of his first steps was to hire Howard Chaykin, a respected graphic artist, to create a poster and comic book series based on the *Star Wars* screenplay. Chaykin designed the artwork in 1976 and it was distributed at science fiction and comic book conventions in the six months prior to the film's release. But although it was produced by Twentieth Century Fox, it includes no reference at all to a movie.

Poster 1   1st Edition Artist: Howard Chaykin **Luke Skywalker** © The Star Wars Corporation 1976

Star Wars (1976)
US 29 × 20 in. (74 × 51 cm)
(Poster Number 1)
Art by Howard Chaykin
Courtesy of the Martin Bridgewater Collection

Star Wars (Gwiezdne Wojny) (1977)
Polish 38 × 27 in. (97 × 69 cm)
Art by Jakub Erol
Courtesy of The Reel Poster Gallery

Return Of The Jedi (Powrot Jedi) (1983)
Polish 38 × 27 in. (97 × 69 cm)
(Style B)
Art by Witold Dybowski
Courtesy of The Reel Poster Gallery

Eastern European film posters have a distinctive and unique style. This is exemplified in Jakub Erol's *Star Wars* poster and in Witold Dybowski's design for *Return Of The Jedi*. Interestingly, Erol chose to illustrate only C-3PO. This is in contrast to other posters, which generally show a montage of characters. Dybowski's exploding head is a metaphor for the destruction of the Empire and Darth Vader's eleventh-hour redemption at the climax of *Return Of The Jedi*.

The American style A poster, also known as the 'Gone With The Wind' style, was withdrawn after a dispute over its omission of Billy Dee Williams. Another poster was thus commissioned that included the actor.

The Empire Strikes Back (1980)
US 41 × 27 in. (104 × 69 cm)
(Style A)
Art by Rodger Kastel
Courtesy of The Reel Poster Gallery

Star Wars: Episode 1 – The Phantom Menace (1999)
US 40 × 27 in. (102 × 69 cm)
Art by Drew Struzan
Courtesy of the Andy Johnson Collection

Star Wars: Episode 1 – The Phantom Menace (1999)
US 40 × 27 in. (102 × 69 cm)
(Advance Style A)
Courtesy of the Andy Johnson Collection

Drew Struzan (b. 1946) graduated with honours from the Art Center College of Design in California and quickly gained a reputation as an illustrator of album covers. Struzan's move into Hollywood came in the late seventies when he was invited to co-design the Style D poster for *Star Wars* with Charles White III (also an Art Center graduate). While White painted the gadgets and spaceships, Struzan used his gift for portraiture to illustrate the characters. This poster launched a love affair between Struzan and *Star Wars* and he is one of an elite list of artists whose name has become synonymous with the films. Stuzan has also worked on the re-release posters for the film and on the new prequel trilogy, designing the main American campaign poster. His other film posters include *Indiana Jones And The Temple Of Doom* (1984) and *Back To The Future* (1985).

The original title of the third *Star Wars* film was *Revenge Of The Jedi*. This was deemed too threatening for a family audience, and it was also argued that a true Jedi would never seek revenge. The movie was thus retitled *Return Of The Jedi*.

Revenge Of The Jedi (1983)
US 41 × 27 in. (104 × 69 cm)
(Second Advance)
Art by Drew Struzan
Courtesy of the Andy Johnson Collection

Tron was the first film to exploit the science fiction possibilities of computers and video games. Prescient for the early eighties, it looked forward to developments in virtual reality and a world that has become obsessed with, and dependent upon, technology. The film used cutting-edge special effects and was an obvious influence on *The Matrix* (1999).

Tron (1982)
US 41 × 27 in. (104 × 69 cm)
(International / Spanish Language)
Courtesy of the Andy Johnson Collection

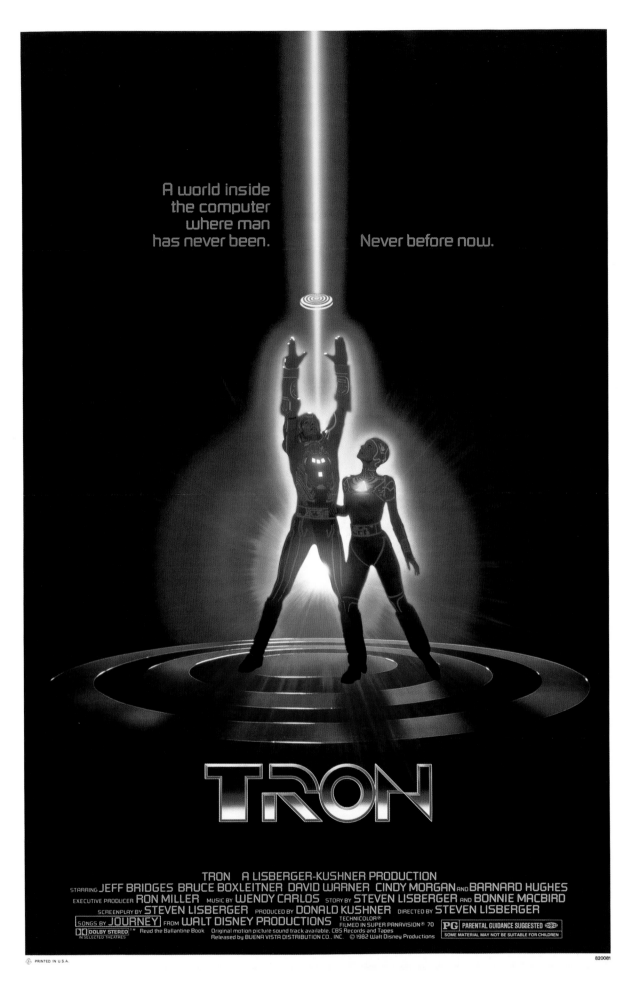

Tron (1982)
US 41 × 27 in. (104 × 69 cm)
Courtesy of the James Lavelle Collection

Johnny Mnemonic (1995)
US 41 × 27 in. (104 × 69 cm)
Art direction and design by Mia Matson
Photo by Gregg Gorman

The cyberpunk film *Johnny Mnemonic* is based on the science-fiction short story by William Gibson. The setting is the near future, where reliance on technology has led to half the world's population suffering from a new disease known as Nerve Attenuation Syndrome (NAS). Keanu Reeves plays Johnny, a data carrier who has the cure for NAS accidentally downloaded into the microchip in his head. This makes him a target for international criminals and he battles to deliver the information before he is either murdered or killed by 'neural seepage' in his brain.

Four years later, Reeves played the lead in another virtual reality film, *The Matrix*. Using state-of-the-art special effects, the film is an action thriller about a computer hacker, Neo, who discovers that 'reality' is in fact an elaborate computer program established by an artificial intelligence system. Neo joins other resistance fighters, led by Morpheus, who believe that Neo is 'The One', the eagerly awaited prophet who can finally crack the Matrix' code and liberate humanity. The poster for *The Matrix*, like that for *Johnny Mnemonic*, reflects the futuristic technologies of the film. Two blockbuster sequels to *The Matrix* were released in 2003.

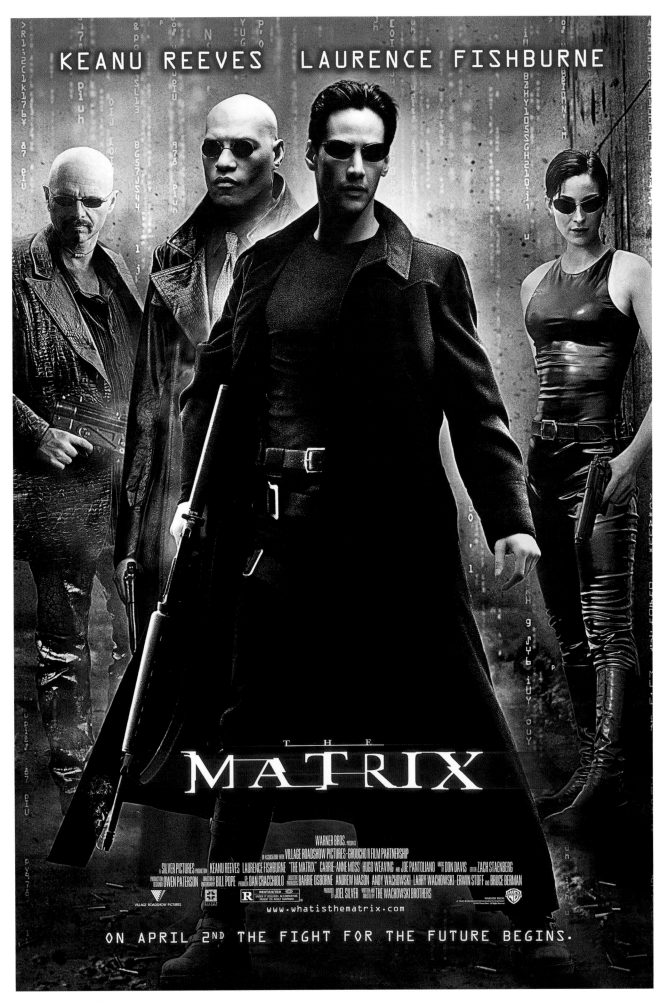

The Matrix (1999)
US 41 × 27 in. (104 × 69 cm)
Courtesy of the John Goddard Collection

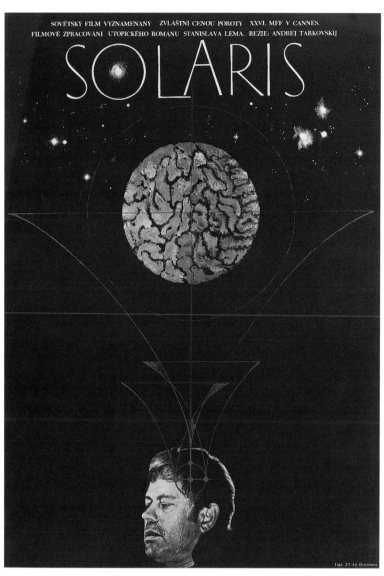

Solaris (1972)
Czechoslovakian 33 × 23 in. (84 × 58 cm)
Courtesy of the Martin Bridgewater Collection

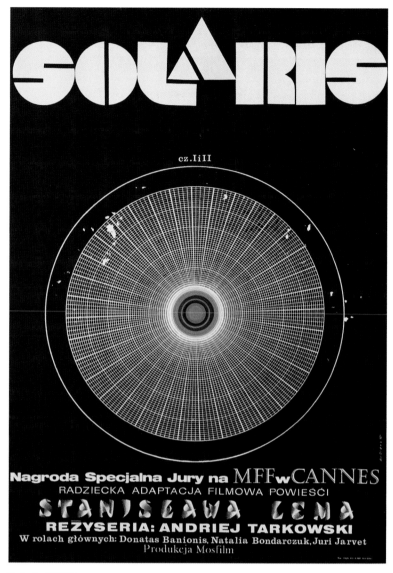

Solaris (1972)
Polish 33 × 23 in. (84 × 58 cm)
Art by Andrzej Bertrandt
Courtesy of the James Moores Collection

Based on the novel by Stanislaw Lem, Andrei Tarkovsky's *Solaris* is a hypnotic magnum opus of Russian cinema. The story follows Banionis, a psychologist who is sent to a space station orbiting a mysterious planet in order to investigate the strange behaviour of the crew. He discovers that the planet is, in fact, a sentient being that is interfering with the crew's memories and forcing them to act out and reveal their hidden obsessions. Banionis himself falls under the being's influence with the result that his dead wife reappears and he is forced to confront his own past. A complex and slow-moving film, *Solaris* can be appreciated and analyzed on many levels. It is a disturbing tale that explores insanity, love and death, and the dangers of trying to bury the past.

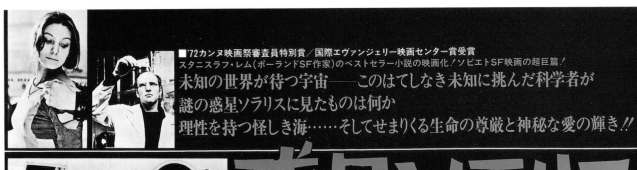

Solaris (1972)
Japanese 30 × 20 in. (76 × 51 cm)
Courtesy of the Martin Bridgewater Collection

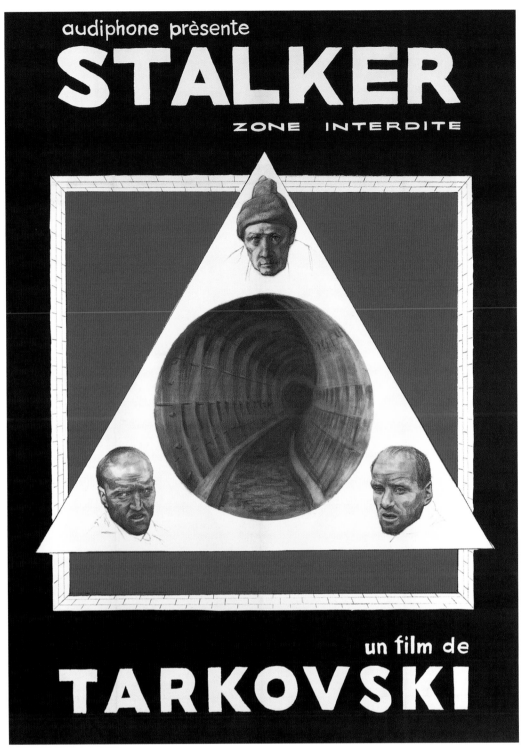

Stalker (1979)
French 63 × 47 in. (160 × 119 cm)
(Style B)
Art by Bougrine
Courtesy of The Reel Poster Gallery

Stalker is another Tarkovsky masterpiece and is as rich in symbolism and layered meaning as his earlier *Solaris*. Two men are on a desperate search for enlightenment. Their goal is The Room, a Mecca that can only be reached by first traversing a vast and dangerous wilderness known as The Zone. The central character, The Stalker, leads the other two men on their long and arduous journey, taking them by an indirect route at a maddeningly slow pace. As they creep forward towards their goal, each of the three men is forced to confront his own desires and doubts and to question his motives for undertaking this pilgrimage.

Jean Michel Folon's poster artwork stresses the allegorical nature and dreamlike qualities of the film. Born in Brussels in 1934, he started out in architecture, before giving up his studies in favour of the more expressive art of illustration. By the sixties he had moved to Paris and was working for a number of magazines and books. Two of his most famous cover illustrations are for Kafka's *Metamorphosis* and Ray Bradbury's *The Martian Chronicles*. He also sold much of his work overseas and his portfolio includes work for *Esquire*, *New Yorker* and *Time*. He designed the French poster for Woody Allen's *Purple Rose Of Cairo* (1985) and has also designed many posters for the Cannes Film Festival. Exhibitions of his work have toured around the world and he is comfortable working in many media, including sculpture, printmaking and etching.

Stalker (1979)
French 63 × 47 in. (160 × 119 cm)
(Style A)
Art by Jean Michel Folon
Courtesy of The Reel Poster Gallery

Aelita (1924)
Russian 28 × 42 in. (72 × 106 cm)
Art by Bograd
Courtesy of the Susan Pack Collection

In the immediate aftermath of the Bolsheviks' seizure of power in 1917, Russia saw a dramatic increase in the arts, especially in the cinema, which quickly became the most popular form of entertainment. The silent films of the day broke many barriers and had a universal appeal in a country where a wide variety of languages were spoken and a third of the population was illiterate. Lenin himself believed that cinema was the most important of the arts and that it could also provide the government with an important tool for spreading propaganda. The industry was nationalized in 1919 and enjoyed a short period of artistic freedom in the twenties, before Stalin began to impose strict controls that reflected his own conviction that art had no purpose other than serving the Party and the state. Like the film industry itself, poster production was centralized under state control and many of the posters from this period were designed by just a handful of artists. Although the designs vary, the posters share many common characteristics derived from the work of contemporary constructivist artists. Montage was very popular, as was the use of angular, architectural forms, bold colours and concentric rings.

Aelita was Russia's first science fiction film (the genre was never a popular one in the Soviet Union) and was both a reaction to and a parody of the films coming out of the West. The plot centres on a Soviet inventor who dreams that he lands on Mars. He finds the planet ruled by Queen Aelita and helps the enslaved population to overthrow her dictatorship in a communist-style revolt – the film's political message was untainted by subtlety. The futuristic designs in *Aelita* influenced subsequent American science fiction films, including *Flash Gordon*.

A Journey To Mars (Puteshestvie Na Mars) (c.1920s)
Russian 40 × 29 in. (102 × 74 cm)
Art by Nikolai Prusakov and Grigori Borisov
Courtesy of the Susan Pack Collection

Death Ray is one of the most brilliant and intelligent Russian films of the period. Funny, tense and fast-paced, it made use of a number of innovative, experimental techniques. The plot, with its obligatory political message, is based on the idea of the proletariat overcoming a dictatorial regime with the help of a death ray.

Luch Smerti (Death Ray) (1925)
Russian 43 × 28 in. (108 × 71 cm)
Art by Anton Lavinsky
Courtesy of the Susan Pack Collection

Luch Smerti (Death Ray) (1925)
Russian 38 × 28 in. (97 × 71 cm)
Art by Alexander Rodchenko
Courtesy of the Susan Pack Collection

Deluge (1933)
US 81 × 41 in. (206 × 104 cm)

Deluge is one of the earliest talkies and is also one of the first 'disaster' flicks. Devastating earthquakes begin hitting America and the destruction climaxes with the annihilation of New York by a tidal wave. The rest of the film focuses on the aftermath of the disaster and one man's struggle to rebuild his life and forget the past.

When Worlds Collide was first published by Philip Wylie and Edwin Balmer in 1932 and although considered for the screen at the time, it was not adapted until 1951. The plot is set in a future where it has been discovered that another planet is on a collision course with Earth and humanity must select a chosen few to survive the Earth's obliteration and start a new life on another planet.

Both *Deluge* and *When Worlds Collide* deal with disaster scenarios that are hypothetically possible. This obsession with the ultimate 'what if?' remains as popular as ever; witness the recent success of films like *Armageddon* (1998) and *Deep Impact* (1998).

When Worlds Collide (1951)
US 41 × 27 in. (104 × 69 cm)

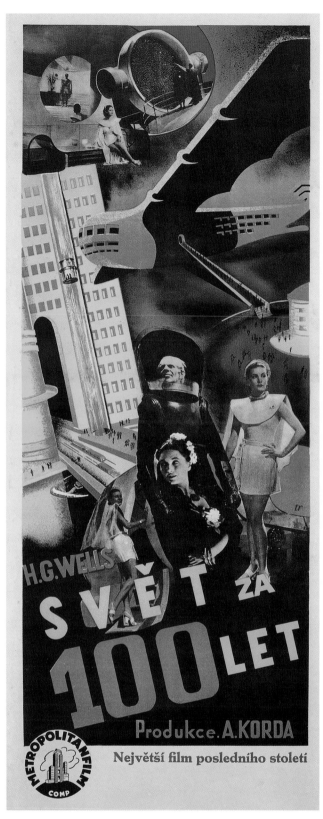

Things To Come (Svet Za 100 Let) (1936)
Czechoslovakian 38 × 12 in. (97 × 30 cm)
Courtesy of the Philip Masheter Collection

Things To Come is one of the most important and self-confident science fiction films in the history of cinema. It was adapted by H. G. Wells from his own book, *The Shape Of Things To Come* (1933), and he promoted it as Britain's answer to *Metropolis* (1926), a film he had despised. Directed by William Cameron Menzies, the film is a lavish epic spanning an entire century. The story opens in 1940 with the outbreak of war. The cinematography, particularly the use of *chiaroscuro* in the war sequences, is arresting, realistic and, as we can see with hindsight, prophetic. The war continues until the 1960s when a plague wipes out most of the world's population. Only pockets of survivors remain, yet from these ashes a new society emerges and thrives by putting its faith in technological and scientific advancement. The film then moves forward to 2036, when the inhabitants of this prosperous utopia are on the eve of sending the first manned flight to the moon, only to find these plans are threatened by a popular uprising against continued technological progress. However, the film ends with the triumph of the two central characters, who are launched into space to begin a new world. The film concludes with the question, 'All the universe ... or nothing. Which shall it be?'

Things To Come (1936)
US 81 × 81 in. (206 × 206 cm)

Things To Come (Nel 2000 Guerra O Pace? (Vita Futura)) (1936)
Italian 55 × 39 in. (140 × 99 cm)
(Re-release 1953)
Courtesy of The Reel Poster Gallery

Things To Come is basically a debate about the role of science in history. Wells believed that the fear of scientific progress had been a root cause of many past wars and he predicted that history would repeat itself in the future unless people were persuaded to embrace, rather than resist, a process which he saw as both irresistible and beneficial. Indeed, he believed that the world could only live in harmony when ruled by a scientific elite. The film concludes with the message that although fear of change is understandable, such fear is ultimately misguided, and that humanity should discard its doubts and strive wholeheartedly to better itself.

Things To Come (1936)
British 30 × 20 in. (76 × 51 cm)
(British Premiere Poster)
Courtesy of the Philip Masheter Collection

The War Of The Worlds (1953)
British 30 × 40 in. (76 × 102 cm)
Courtesy of the Andrew Cohen Collection

The War Of The Worlds (1953)
US 81 × 41 in. (206 × 104 cm)
(Re-Release 1965)
Courtesy of the Steve Smith Collection

H. G. Wells (1866–1946) wrote well over one hundred books, including fifty novels. He was one of the early pioneers in the field of science fiction and his work in the genre includes four of his best-known novels: *The Time Machine* (1895), *The Invisible Man* (1897), *The War Of The Worlds* (1898) and *The Shape Of Things To Come* (1933), all of which have been made into classic science fiction films. *The War Of The Worlds* was written at a time when the American astronomer Percival Lowell was claiming that he had observed 'canals' on Mars and there was much speculation about the possibility of life beyond our planet. Whereas the novel is a thinly disguised parable about the cruelty of nineteenth-century colonialism, which has the Martians landing in the English Home Counties, the film, released in 1953, transplants the Martian invasion to the US and reflects contemporary fears about a war with communist Russia. The film's success was in part due to memories of the public panic that had been created by Orson Welles' famous radio broadcast of the tale in 1938.

Like Jules Verne, Wells had an almost uncanny knack for prediction, forecasting many inventions, from dishwashers to aeroplanes. He accurately envisaged the advent of a consumer society in which large highways would carry an endless stream of automobiles and people would live in pre-fabricated houses full of labour-saving gadgetry. When he turned to political prediction, he argued that capitalism and the nation state would collapse under the strain of devastating wars. This forecast came close to being realized in the First World War, and Wells lived on to see the dropping of the first atomic bombs in August 1945, a development he had predicted thirty years previously.

The War Of The Worlds (1953)
US 41 × 27 in. (104 × 69 cm)

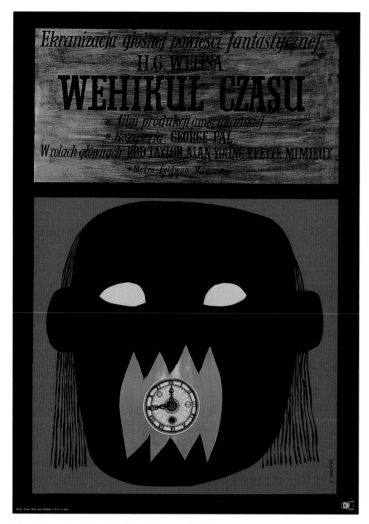

The Time Machine (Wehikul Czasu) (1960)
Polish 33 × 23 in. (84 × 58 cm)
Art by Marian Stachurski
Courtesy of The Reel Poster Gallery

The Time Machine (1960)
US 40 × 30 in. (102 × 74 cm)
Art by Reynold Brown
Courtesy of The Reel Poster Gallery

● **1859.** Charles Darwin publishes *The Origin Of Species*, setting out his theory that all living species are a product of evolution and not, as previously believed, the result of a seven-day creation.

● **1905.** Einstein discovers his Theory of Relativity, which implies, among much else, that time travel is in theory, if not as yet in practice, possible. Clocks do, in fact, slow down as you approach the speed of light.

The Time Machine is an adaptation of H. G. Wells' classic novel first published in 1895. George builds a time machine and travels into the future, only to find himself in a world riven by bitter warfare and, reaching 1966, he witnesses the destruction of London in a nuclear explosion. He then travels thousands of years into the future in the hope of reaching a point at which people have abandoned their warlike ways. However, when he does arrive at a period of apparent peace, it is only to find that humanity is now controlled by the Morlocks – a flesh-eating sub-species of homosapiens that has evolved during the long, dark centuries of war. These creatures capture George's machine and he must challenge them if he is to return to his own time. The film obviously reflects the ideas of Social Darwinism that were in vogue when Wells was writing his novel, and accurately reflects his anxiety to warn his readers that human progress is not inevitable and to alert them to the need to do something now to avert future catastrophe.

The Time Machine (L' Uomo Che Visse Nel Futuro) (1960)
Italian 79 × 55 in. (201 × 140 cm)
Art by Silvano Campeggi (Nano)

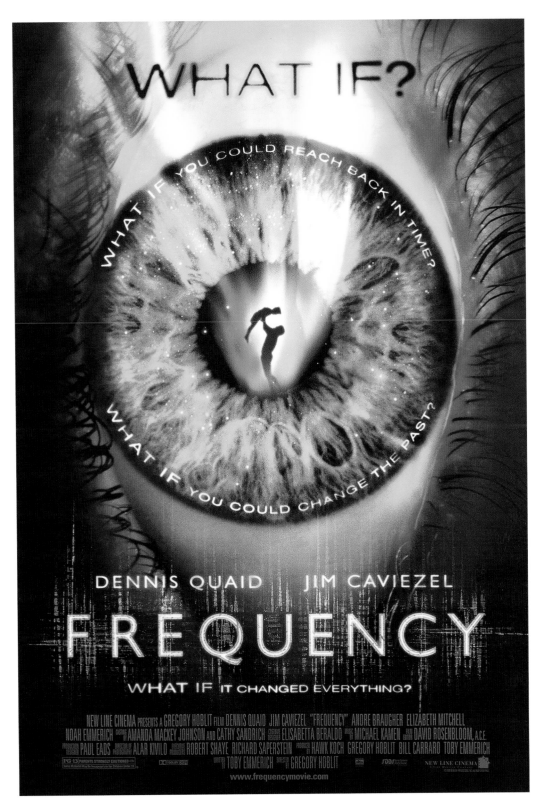

Frequency (2000)
US 41 × 27 in. (104 × 69 cm)
Courtesy of the Andy Johnson Collection

Back To The Future is an amusing look at the confusion and complications that result from interfering with time. A nostalgic and crazy fantasy, the film was one of the top grossing movies of the eighties and Struzan's artwork is also one of the most memorable posters from the decade. Like *Back To The Future*, *Frequency* is another convoluted tale that centres on the confusing consequences of time trave.

Back To The Future (1985)
US 41 × 27 in. (104 × 69 cm)
Art by Drew Struzan
Courtesy of The Reel Poster Gallery

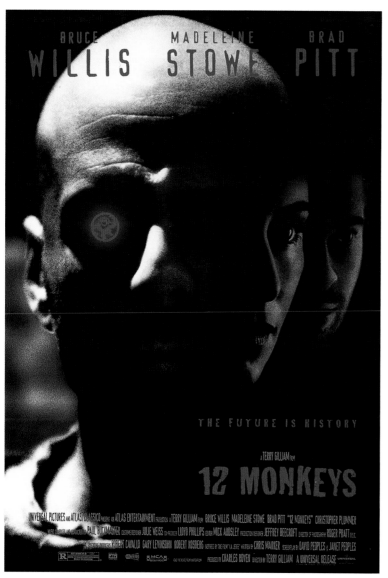

12 Monkeys (1995)
US 41 × 27 in. (104 × 69 cm)
Photo by Phillip Caruso
Art direction by Evan Wright
Courtesy of the Andy Johnson Collection

12 Monkeys (1995)
US 41 × 27 in. (104 × 69 cm)
(International)
Photo by Phillip Caruso
Design by Brian Bysouth & Steve Reeves
Courtesy of the Sean Lee Collection

Terry Gilliam's *12 Monkeys* is a disturbing tale set in both the present and the near future. A surreal and paranoid film, *12 Monkeys* was inspired by the tour de force short *La jetée* by Chris Marker, a prominent figure of the French New Wave.

12 Monkeys (1995)
US 41 × 27 in. (104 × 69 cm)
(Advance)
Concept by Terry Gilliam and R. Scott Purcell
Logo design by BLT & Associates
Courtesy of the Andy Johnson Collection

TWO YEARS IN THE MAKING!

DESTINATION MOON

COLOR BY TECHNICOLOR

Produced by GEORGE PAL · Directed by IRVING PICHEL
Screenplay by RIP VAN RONKEL, ROBERT HEINLEIN and JAMES O'HANLON

Destination Moon (1950)
US 41 × 27 in. (104 × 69 cm)

The fifties was a nervous decade in America. The Cold War was at its height and the United States and Soviet Russia were engaged in a race for nuclear superiority. Towards the end of the decade, the introduction of the first intercontinental missiles and the launch of Sputnik would focus attention on the military potential of space. But as the decade began, audiences were already fascinated by the promise of space exploration. *Destination Moon* (1950) reflects this interest and details the story of the first manned American mission to the moon, which succeeds despite opposition from 'Anti-American' forces. The film's makers studied the very latest advances in technology in order to create a highly realistic rocketship. The film won an Academy Award for Special Effects.

- **1957, 4 October.** Sputnik 1, the first man-made earth satellite, is launched by the USSR.
- **1958, 1 October.** NASA is founded, taking over the role of the National Advisory Committee on Aeronautics.
- **1959, 12 September.** Luna 2, the first man-made object to reach the moon, is launched by the USSR.
- **1960, 18 August.** The USA launches its first spy satellite.
- **1961, 12 April.** Yuri A. Gagarin of the USSR becomes the first man in space. He orbits Earth once.
- **1969, 20 July.** Neil Armstrong of the USA becomes the first man to set foot on the moon.

Destination Moon (Uomini Sulla Luna) (1950)
Italian 55 × 39 in. (140 × 99 cm)

Star Trek: The Motion Picture (Star Trek) (1979)
East German 33 × 23 in. (84 × 58 cm)
Art by Regine Schulz and Burckhard Labowski
Courtesy of The Reel Poster Gallery

Gene Roddenberry's *Star Trek* is a phenomenon and a franchise. Fans devoted to the exploits of the *USS Enterprise* and her crew flock to websites and conventions around the world and the original television series has given birth to four spin-off series and numerous feature films. The first of these films, simply titled *Star Trek: The Motion Picture*, which premièred in 1979, was made after Paramount Pictures scrapped plans for a second series of *Star Trek* and the two-hour pilot was converted for the big screen. The film has all the hallmarks of the original series: a classic science fiction setting, pertinent social comment and likeable characters. Indeed, the film's success relied to a considerable degree on the popularity of the actors who played the central roles and this is reflected in the poster designs. The image in the unusual East German poster is instantly recognizable as Leonard Nimoy in the role of Spock. Similarly, the likenesses of Nimoy and William Shatner are unmistakable on Bob Peak's artwork.

Star Trek: The Motion Picture (1979)
US 41 × 27 in. (104 × 69 cm)
Art by Bob Peak
Courtesy of The Reel Poster Gallery

Terrore Nello Spazio (Planet Of The Vampires) (1965)
Italian 28 × 13 in. (71 × 33 cm)
Art by Averardo Ciriello
Courtesy of The Reel Poster Gallery

It! The Terror From Beyond Space (1958) (see p. 4) and *Terrore Nello Spazio* had a direct influence on Ridley Scott's *Alien* (1979). In *It!* a spaceship returns from Mars with the crew all dead, except for a sole survivor who is accused of the murder of his crewmates. However, he denies the charge, claiming that the killings are the work of a Martian monster. To establish the truth of his claim, a second mission is launched and the crew of this ship again meet a grisly fate at the hands of a parasitic monster that feeds on human flesh. *Terrore Nello Spazio* is the work of the noted Italian director Mario Bava, and the cinematography is both beautiful and eerie. The similarities with *Alien* are again striking. This time, a crew of astronauts, attracted to an unexplored planet by strange radio signals, find an ancient spaceship together with the remains of ancient aliens and soon find that they are being stalked by a mysterious and deadly presence. Averardo Ciriello's artwork of a spaceship racing towards a chilling face in the nebula encapsulates the menace and horror of the film.

Terrore Nello Spazio (Planet Of The Vampires) (1965)
Italian 79 × 55 in. (201 × 140 cm)
Art by Averardo Ciriello
Courtesy of The Reel Poster Gallery

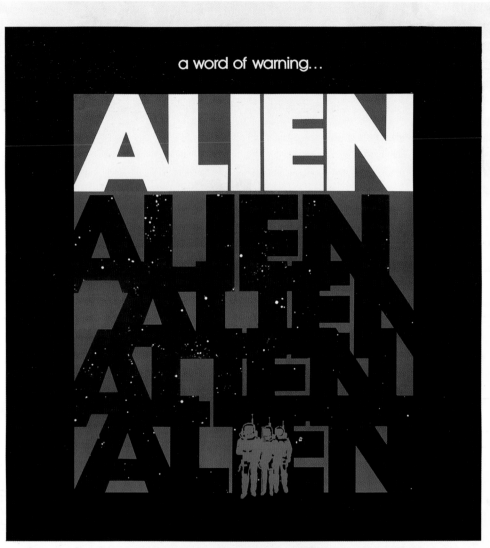

Steve Frankfurt, the winner of the 1995 Hollywood Reporter Key Art Lifetime Achievement Award, has a gift for producing sound bites that capture the essence of a film in just a few words. The taglines that he has created for endless film campaigns have become almost as famous as the films themselves. It was Frankfurt who asked us to 'Pray for Rosemary's Baby' (*Rosemary's Baby*, 1968), reminded us that 'Every father's daughter is a virgin' (*Goodbye Columbus*, 1969) and allowed us to 'Feel good, without feeling bad' (*Emmanuelle*, 1974). His tagline for *Alien* (1979) was equally effective, expressing the horror of the film without giving anything away. 'In space, no one can hear you scream' not only helped *Alien* become one of the most successful horror films ever, it has also become a familiar, everyday expression.

Alien (1979)
US 41 × 27 in. (104 × 69 cm)
(Advance)
Design by Steve Frankfurt
Courtesy of the Martin Bridgewater Collection

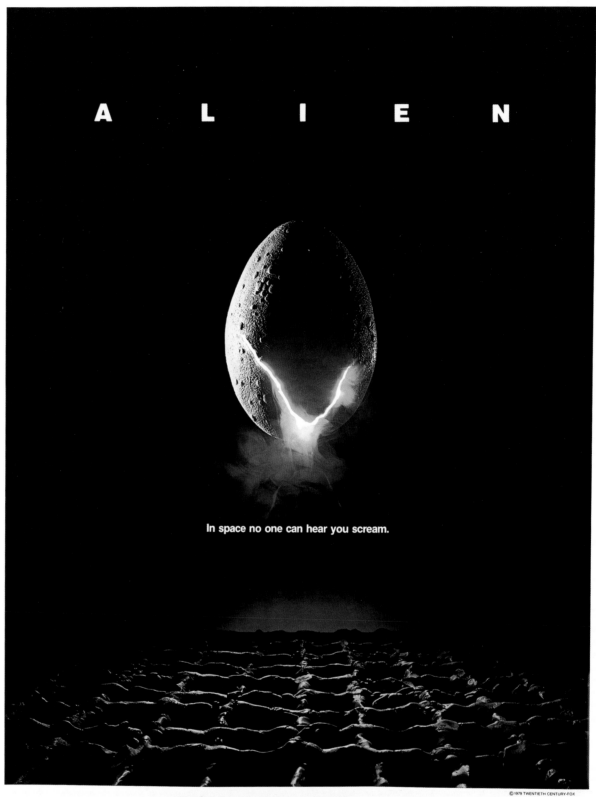

Alien (1979)
US 41 × 27 in. (104 × 69 cm)
Art by Philip Gips
Design by Steve Frankfurt
Courtesy of The Reel Poster Gallery

Flight To Mars (1951)
US 81 × 41 in. (206 × 104 cm)

Mars has always had an irresistible allure for both writers of science fiction and their readers. This may be because its relative proximity to Earth means that it is quite conceivable that people may one day visit the red planet. *Flight To Mars* tells the story of one such trip, in which (surprise, surprise) the astronauts encounter both evil and benevolent Martians.

Capricorn One offers a much more 'realistic' version of man's first flight to Mars. In this scenario, the world watches as the first manned rocket is launched to the red planet. But what the public don't know is that the astronauts are not actually aboard the spacecraft at all; instead they have been blackmailed into transmitting recordings of their mission from a film studio in the middle of the desert. When the rocket crashes on its return to Earth, however, the astronauts become 'officially' dead and they are forced to fight for their lives against a government desperate to prevent the public from discovering that it has been deceived. *Capricorn One* is a fast-paced conspiracy film, culminating in a breathtaking finale, which was obviously inspired by the ideas of a lunatic fringe of conspiracy theorists who believe that Neil Armstrong never, in fact, landed on the moon.

Capricorn One (1978)
British 41 × 27 in. (104 × 69 cm)
(Style B)
Art by Kelly
Courtesy of the Bruce Marchant Collection

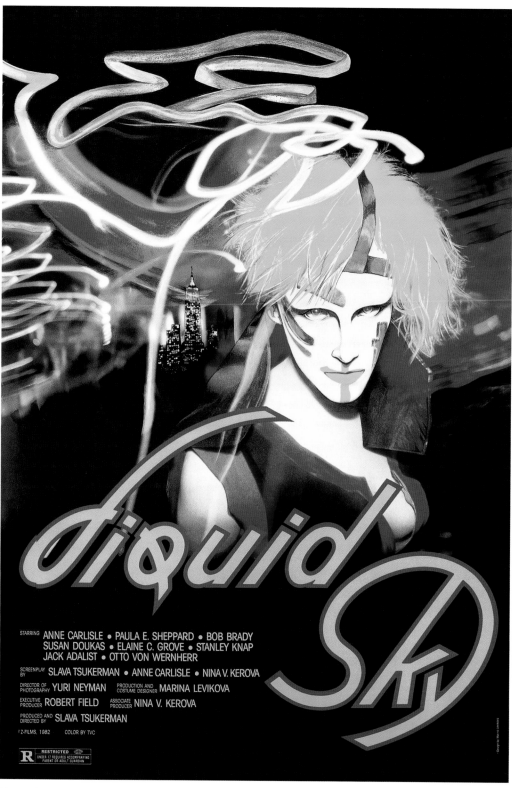

Liquid Sky (1982)
US 36 × 25 in. (91 × 64 cm)
Art by Marina Levikova
Courtesy of The Reel Poster Gallery

Liquid Sky and *Dune* are among the more hallucinatory science-fiction films of the eighties. Although they share a dreamlike quality, the two films are distinctly different in style and content. *Liquid Sky* has been described as 'Andy Warhol's Trash with aliens' and is a protest against the desperation and ugliness of life. In contrast, *Dune* is a complex fantasy set in the distant future of 10191. Adapted from the book by Frank Herbert, the film is set against a backdrop of interstellar warfare between rival feudal kingdoms.

Renato Casaro (b. 1935) was born in Italy and showed an interest in the art of cinema from childhood. At the age of seventeen he undertook to paint the façade of his local cinema in exchange for free tickets. He moved to Rome during the war and stayed on to work for Studio Favalli, the largest and most prestigious advertising agency for the movie industry at that time. But it was in the sixties that Casaro's work was first brought to an international audience when his poster for *The Bible* (1965) was displayed on Hollywood's Sunset Boulevard and elsewhere across the world. Since then, he has worked on a number of poster campaigns in Europe and has received several awards for his art. His style combines a unique use of acrylic and tempera paint with an airbrush finish.

Dune (1984)
British 41 × 27 in. (104 × 69 cm)
Art by Renato Casaro
Courtesy of the Martin Bridgewater Collection

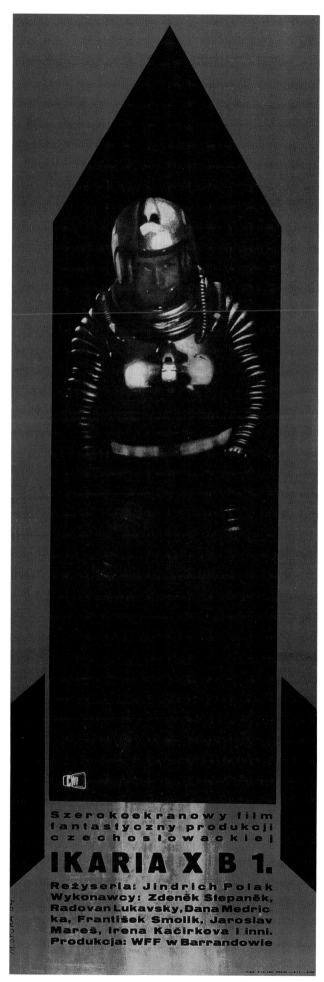

Ikaria XB1 (Voyage To The End Of The Universe) (1963)
Polish 33 × 11 in. (84 × 28 cm)
Art by Maria Syska
Courtesy of The Reel Poster Gallery

Ikaria XB1 (1963) is a little known Czechoslovakian film of the early sixties. A huge spaceship is on a long voyage into deep space when the crew encounters a deserted craft and a mysterious nebula. One man starts to go insane and jeopardizes both the mission and the crew. The film predates and anticipates many subsequent developments in American science fiction. The trans-galactic ship, carrying a whole community across space, is very similar to the *Enterprise* in *Star Trek* and the encounter with the deserted craft foreshadows Ridley Scott's *Alien*. Most comparisons have been made, however, with *2001: A Space Odyssey*. The lavish interiors of the spaceship evoke images from Kubrick's space-station and the concept of a central computer that controls the crew reminds us of *HAL 9000*, the computer that malfunctions in *2001*.

Stanley Kubrick's science-fiction symphony, *2001: A Space Odyssey* marked a science fiction watershed and remains a highly influential work. With his cinematic meditation on humanity, beauty, art and science, Kubrick changed the concept of what a film could and should be. The film's enigmatic message and the hallucinatory quality of its imagery were welcomed by an audience drawn from the youthful, drug-taking counterculture, eager to distance itself from an older generation that simply did not understand what Kubrick was trying to convey. Two years in the making, *2001* is science fiction in its purest form. Based on the very latest technological advances, it has some of the most stunning visual effects ever created. The grandeur and vastness of space is conveyed with a dramatic realism that is enhanced by the rousing classical music used as a backdrop for the film.

Wiktor Gorka (b. 1922) graduated from the Warsaw Academy of Fine Arts in 1952. He has toured exhibitions of his work around the world and has won numerous awards. Three of his most famous designs are the Polish posters for *Spartacus* (1960), *2001: A Space Odyssey* (1968) and *Cabaret* (1972).

2001: A Space Odyssey (2001 Odyseja Kosmiczna) (1968)
Polish 33 × 23 in. (84 × 58 cm)
Art by Wiktor Gorka
Courtesy of The Reel Poster Gallery

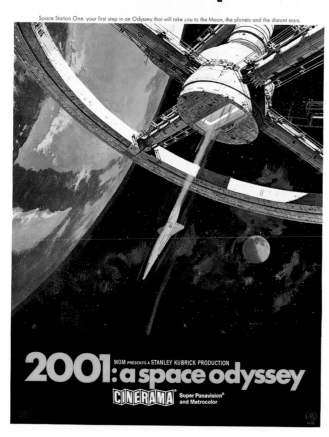

An epic drama of adventure and exploration

Space Station One: your first step in an Odyssey that will take you to the Moon, the planets and the distant stars.

2001: a space odyssey
MGM PRESENTS A STANLEY KUBRICK PRODUCTION
CINERAMA Super Panavision® and Metrocolor

2001: A Space Odyssey (1968)
US 60 × 40 in. (152 × 102 cm)
(Style A Cinerama)
Art by Robert T. McCall
Courtesy of The Reel Poster Gallery

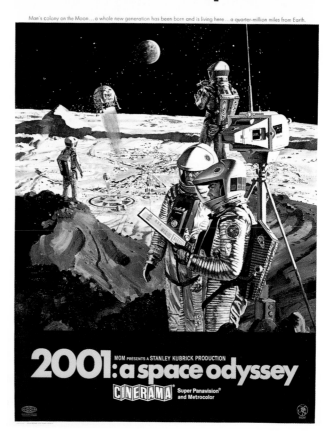

An epic drama of adventure and exploration

Man's colony on the Moon...a whole new generation has been born and is living here...a quarter-million miles from Earth.

2001: a space odyssey
MGM PRESENTS A STANLEY KUBRICK PRODUCTION
CINERAMA Super Panavision® and Metrocolor

2001: A Space Odyssey (1968)
US 41 × 27 in. (104 × 69 cm)
(Style B Cinerama)
Art by Robert T. McCall
Courtesy of the Martin Pope Collection

Robert T. McCall (b. 1919) is America's foremost space artist and his multi-storey murals are displayed at the National Air and Space Museum in Washington, DC, at the Johnson Space Center in Texas and at the Flight Research Center in California. After studying at Colombus College of Art and Design and the Art Institute of Chicago, McCall worked as an artist in the Army Air Corps during World War II, focusing his attention on aeronautical subjects. After the war, his interest in this field expanded to include the developing field of space exploration and it was a series of his paintings on space in *Life* magazine in the late fifties that first caught the attention of NASA. He was one of the first American artists commissioned to document the Agency's history and he is still involved in this project today. This love affair with space continued in 1967 when he worked with Stanley Kubrick on the poster campaign for *2001: A Space Odyssey*. McCall works mainly in oils and his work combines imagination with a great attention to detail. In 1988 he was inducted into the Illustrator's Hall of Fame.

In the 1960s only a small selection of cinemas had the capacity to show films shot in Cinerama. Special posters were printed for these screenings, displaying the Cinerama logo. When Cinerama films were later put on general release, the posters would be reprinted but without the logo. The American Style C poster is the only design from the original Cinerama campaign for *2001: A Space Odyssey* not to be used for the film's general release.

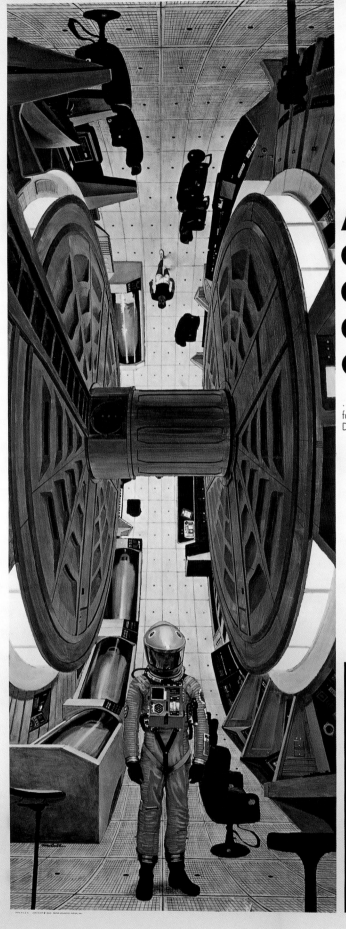

An epic
drama of
adventure
and
exploration

...taking you half a billion miles from Earth...
further from home than any man in history.
Destination: Jupiter.

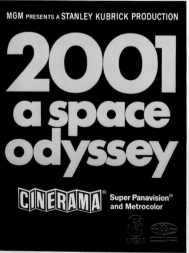

2001: A Space Odyssey (1968)
US 41 × 27 in. (104 × 69 cm)
(Style C Cinerama)
Art by Robert T. McCall
Courtesy of the Andy Johnson Collection

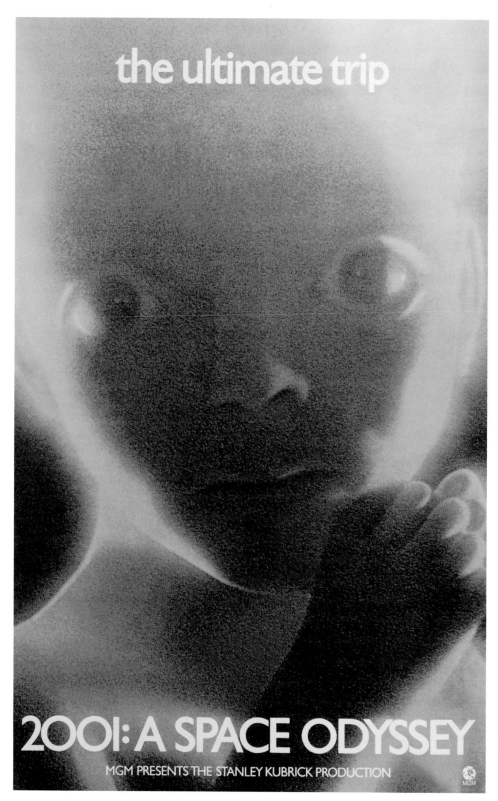

2001: A Space Odyssey (1968/9)
US 41 × 27 in. (104 × 69 cm)
(Style E)
Design by Mike Kaplan
Courtesy of the Andrew MacDonald Collection

The American Style D and Style E posters for *2001: A Space Odyssey* were only used for 'wild' pastings on New York City walls and in subway stations. Mike Kaplan's tagline 'The Ultimate Trip' and the image of the Star Child floating in an iris captured the experimental mood of the time, and struck a chord with audiences. This poster is one of the most evocative of its decade. The Star Child image was used for subsequent re-releases of the film in the 1970s.

Mike Kaplan has worn various hats in the film world: producer, director, actor, distributor, marketeer and avid movie poster collector. As an art director, he has won two Hollywood Reporter Key Art awards, for *Marlene* (1984) and *Welcome to L.A.* (1976). He made his auspicious debut as a designer of posters with the 'Ultimate Trip'/ Star Child campaign for *2001: A Space Odyssey* and went on to create six posters with noted illustrator Philip Castle, beginning with *A Clockwork Orange* and including *The Valley (Obscured By Clouds)* (1972), *The Whales of August* (1987), *Gangster No. 1* (2000) and, most recently, Mike Hodges' *I'll Sleep When I'm Dead* (2004), which he also produced. His posters have incorporated the work of leading contemporary painters, including David Hockney for *A Bigger Splash* (1974), Allen Jones for *Maîtresse* (1976) and ceramic artist Karen Donleavy for *A Wedding* (1978).

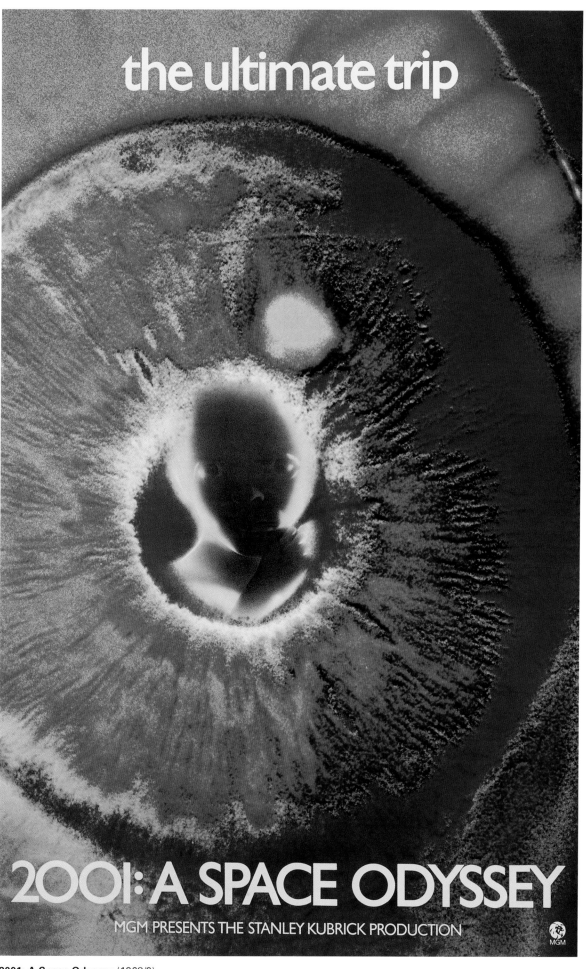

2001: A Space Odyssey (1968/9)
US 41 × 27 in. (104 × 69 cm)
(Style D)
Design by Mike Kaplan
Courtesy of The Reel Poster Gallery

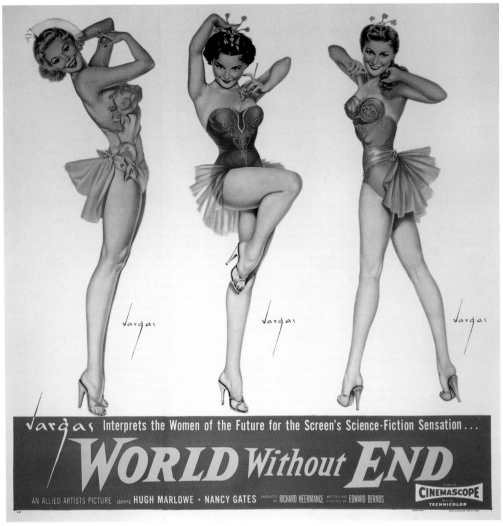

World Without End has all the characteristics of fifties science fiction – giant spiders, evil mutants and girls in short dresses abound. The film is remarkably similar to Wells' *The Time Machine*, and at one point a lawsuit was filed alleging plagiarism from the novel. But in all other respects *World Without End* is a straightforward, unremarkable science fiction film. This cannot be said of the poster design. Alberto Vargas did the production design for the film and was also commissioned to do an alternative, large poster for the American campaign. This featured his famous 'Varga Girls' and is one of the most unusual science fiction poster designs ever created.

World Without End (1956)
US 81 × 81 in. (206 × 206 cm)
(Style B)
Art by Alberto Vargas

Known for his pin-ups and paintings of the female nude, **Alberto Vargas** (1896–1982) was one of America's most famous commercial artists, whose 'Varga Girls' have become American icons. Born in Peru, Vargas moved to New York around the time of the Great War. In the twenties he was the exclusive painter of the Follies Girls for Florenz Ziegfeld – his Ziegfeld Follies were a showcase for the most talented starlets in America. Vargas moved west to Hollywood, where he painted the stars and worked on set designs. In the forties he began work for *Esquire* and during the war the fame of his pin-ups was spread by American soldiers who carried these treasured possessions with them across the world. The US Government recognized the morale-raising role of Vargas' scantily clad young ladies by awarding him an official decoration for his work. In the fifties he did a legendary series of twelve nudes that confirmed his status as one of America's foremost artists and his work for *Playboy* in the sixties and seventies brought him further international acclaim. Few artists, before or since, have been able to capture the beauty and sexuality of the female form like Alberto Vargas.

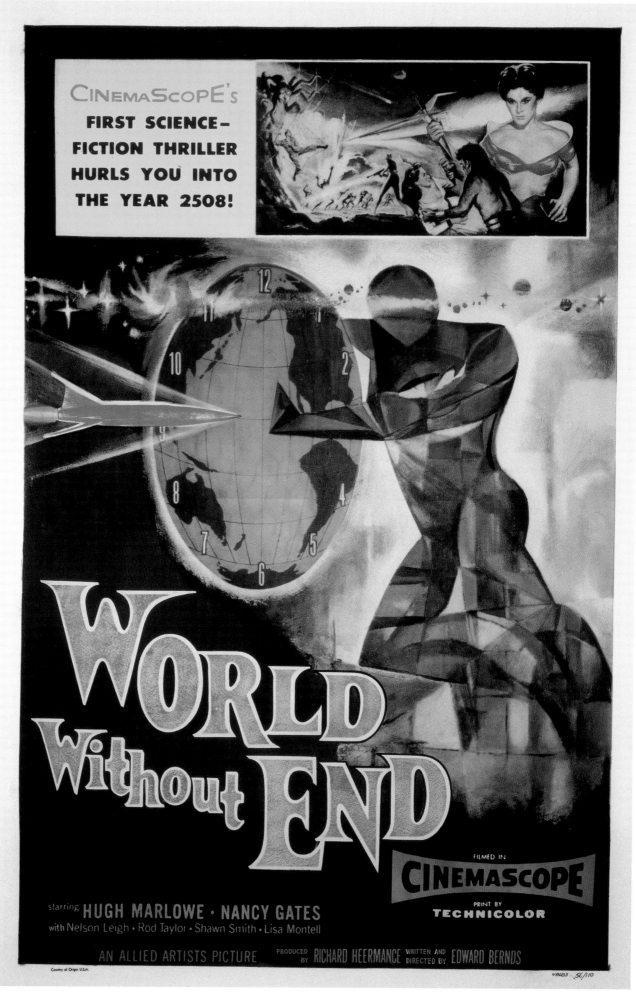

World Without End (1956)
US 41 × 27 in. (104 × 69 cm)

La Naissance Du Cinema Lumière Méliès
(Festival Mondial Du Film Et Des Beaux-Arts De Belgique) (1947)
Belgian 47 × 32 in. (119 × 81 cm)
Art by Félix Labisse
Courtesy of The Reel Poster Gallery

Félix Labisse (1905-1982) was a well-known Belgian surrealist painter. He illustrated a number of books and his most famous works are *The Golden Fleece* and *Medusine*. Labisse was commissioned to design a poster for an exhibition of Méliès' and Lumière's films in Belgium in 1947. He also designed the poster for the exhibition's tour of France.

TITLE INDEX

ARTIST, DESIGNER AND PHOTOGRAPHER INDEX

Until The End Of The World (1991)
British 23 × 50 in. (58 × 127 cm)
Courtesy of The Reel Poster Gallery